Written and illustrated by

Susan Lintell

The
Ninja
Marketing Toolkit

New Generation Publishing

www.newgeneration-publishing.com

2

Earnings Disclaimer

There is no guarantee that you will get any results or earn money using any of the ideas, tools, strategies or recommendations in this book. Nothing in this book is a promise or guarantee of earnings.
Your level of success will be dependent on a number of factors, including:

- Your skills, knowledge and ability
- Your dedication
- Your networking ability and network
- Your business expertise and experience experience
- Your financial situation.

Any statements in this book are our opinions and are not guarantees or promises of actual performance. We make no guarantees that you will achieve any results from the ideas or models presented in this book and we don't offer any professional, legal, medical, psychological or financial advice.

PREFACE

Welcome

Welcome to The Ninja Marketing Toolkit. We hope you're looking forward to exploring our brand new collection of marketing tools and using them to design and implement your own marketing plan. Whether your business is large or small, you're looking for personal development or you just like marketing, we hope that you thoroughly enjoy the journey!

We have designed The Ninja Marketing Toolkit with an original approach to presenting information, using concise text and bullet points in an attractive, digestible format that's fun to use. Our aim is to give you the opportunity to discover the fascinating world of marketing and to give you the knowledge and tools you need to achieve your business, marketing and personal goals.

So, whether you're in business, working in a marketing environment or just want to develop your skills, there'll be plenty for you. You can choose from within our extensive toolkit to equip you to deal with any marketing situation. You don't need a marketing background to understand how to use the toolkit and become a Ninja Marketer, it's practical and fun.

Remember, even a journey of a thousand miles begins with one footstep, so you can start your journey by using The Ninja Marketing Toolkit today!

Enjoy and have fun!

Regards
The Ninja Marketing Team

Arion

Ariella

Akira

Akimi

THE AUTHOR

Susan Lintell
Chartered Marketer, MCIM, FISMM

Susan Lintell is a Chartered Marketer, a member of the Chartered Institute of Marketing (CIM), a fellow of the Institute of Sales and Marketing Management (ISMM) and a member of the Institute of Directors (IOD). She specialises in marketing, marketing communications, social media marketing, business development and telemarketing. She is also a graphic designer, illustrator and cartoonist and was the founder of a successful presentation and production company in central London. Susan has many years of sales and marketing experience.

She has worked for the Chartered Institute of Marketing as a Training Advisor and lectured for the CIM postgraduate qualification. Susan has worked with blue-chip organisations in a variety of sectors, including: financial services, not-for-profit, petrochemicals, management consultancy, training, healthcare, Intellectual Property (IP) and Information Technology (IT).

What is a Ninja 忍者 ?

Ninja were fighters in feudal Japan who were famed for their unusual methods and extreme effectiveness. Their methods can be contrasted with those of the Samurai, whose techniques were more conventional and predictable. Ninja were so effective that they became the stuff of legend, making it difficult to separate fact from fiction. However, it's clear that they excelled in a culture devoted to the pursuit of excellence through training and technical skill.

As Ninja Marketers, we have followed these principles in The Ninja Marketing Toolkit. We designed this handbook to give you an understanding of the significance and practical application of fundamental Ninja marketing skills, so that you can develop and deliver a highly effective marketing plan and become a Ninja Marketer.

Chapter 1 - THE NINJA MARKETING TOOLKIT

1. INTRODUCTION

Our Ninja Marketing tools can save you time and money. You can use them to build your marketing plan, fix a problem, take market share from your competitors, enter new markets and retain and build your existing markets. You just need to know how, when, where and why to use them.

What is The Ninja Marketing Toolkit?

THE NINJA MARKETING TOOLKIT IS...
… A toolkit that gives you practical advice to help you prepare a successful marketing plan. We've included definitions, principles, models, forms and templates and a guide on how to use them, so that you understand the principles of successful marketing and see the big picture.

Why Use The Ninja Marketing Toolkit?

Today's marketing environment is really challenging and marketing is entering a new era, which will make the past look like a picnic. The Ninja Marketing Toolkit helps you stay ahead of the competition and gain a sustainable competitive advantage, because:

It really delivers results,
Which means increased market share and business growth at lower cost

It's cost effective
Which means maximum return for minimum investment

It's focused
Which means you'll work smarter, not harder

It's flexible
Which means adjusting your strategies to the situation, not the opposite

It gives you a competitive edge
Over competitors large and small, everywhere in the world

It enables you to punch above your weight
Which means you'll fight smarter, not harder

2. INTRODUCING THE TEAM

Arion

I'm Arian the lion, known as the brave one in many languages. I'm the team leader and a Master of Ninja Marketing. I specialise in formulating winning strategies and planning awesome tactics that are designed to get ahead of the competition, increase market share and create and defend long-term, sustainable competitive advantage.

Ariella

I'm Ariella, the lioness, Arion's trusted partner and also a Master of Ninja Marketing. Together we are a great team! I'm the Ninja action woman and I effectively carry out the action plans with amazing speed and grace. The competition never knows what's coming next or what's hit them!

Akira

I'm Akira, which means intelligent and enlightened. I'm really shy, quiet and prefer more peaceful pursuits - like analysing data, accounting, planning, research, control and contingency planning. I'd much rather be at my desk with my books, computers and calculators than out there in the marketing environment. I'm here to make sure that the team stays on track.

Akimi

I'm Akimi, Akira's partner, I'm very reserved and serious. It's my job to plan and monitor the timetables and budgets, which I take very seriously. It's also my role to keep the team focused and co-ordinated, by communicating with each member to ensure that everything is going as planned and that everyone is kept in the loop.

3. HOW TO USE THE NINJA MARKETING TOOLKIT

The Ninja Marketing Toolkit can be used in sequence from beginning to end. However, you can start wherever you like or use any of the bite size pieces you need, when you need them. You may notice some repetition of key principles, this is because they are relevant to different elements of the toolkit.

Marketing Tools

Differentiation from Your Competitors

- Define your Unique Selling Propositions (USPs)
- Be better than your competitors – give VIP service
- Be nimble to outwit the competition

Innovation

- Always look for opportunities to innovate
- Focus on innovation and continuous improvement
- Change the rules, redesign the industry, invent new business models
- Don't just respond to market trends, lead them
- Don't just educate your market, create a marketplace
- Be creative and think outside the box

Know Your Customers (KYC)

- Know who your customers are and understand their needs
- Find customers who would love to beat a path to your door, but don't know you exist
- Satisfy the needs of customers who would love to buy your products and services, if only you provided what they need
- Find those customers who buy from the competition or use alternatives
- Find former customers and get them back

- ### Customer Delight
- React quickly to customer needs and market trends
- Deliver fantastic customer service
- Make your customers happy and keep them happy

GREY BOXES – DEFINITIONS AND PRINCIPLES

RED BOXES – PRACTICAL APPLICATIONS, FACTS AND TIPS

Chapter 2 – PLANNING

1. CORPORATE PLANNING

Introduction

At the beginning of the planning process corporate planners, who are responsible for corporate policy, are involved in corporate planning. Marketing and other functions, including sales, finance, HR, production and distribution, need to work together as a team to formulate and implement their own objectives, strategies and tactics that will help to achieve corporate objectives.

THE CORPORATE PLANNING PROCESS

STEP 1   **The Corporate Mission Statement**
The corporate mission statement defines the purpose of your business and should express what your organisation is aiming to achieve. It should focus on your long-term direction and include products, services, markets, customer needs and technology. It should be simple, honest and easy to grasp in order to motivate your staff and fulfill the needs of your customers.

STEP 2   **Corporate Objectives**
The corporate objectives are expressed in financial terms and focus on profitability. They are the foundation on which marketing objectives and plans are built, provide direction and are the standards used for evaluating performance. These objectives need to be SMART: specific, measureable, attainable, realistic and time specific and include turnover, profit, ROI and comparative rates of growth.

STEP 3   **Corporate Strategies**
Corporate strategies are plans for the development of your organisation and are integrated with the strategic plans of all its functions. They will achieve corporate objectives by rethinking and redesigning processes and practices to improve performance in all areas. The goal is to achieve a higher level of competitive advantage, respond to environmental, competitive or other changes and take your organisation to the next level. These strategies include:

Organic Growth
Start and build a new business or grow your existing business

Strategic Alliances and Joint Ventures
Strategic alliances can lower the risks to your business and can be used for specific projects

Mergers and Acquisitions
Join forces with other businesses, buy an existing business or be acquired by a larger organisation

Culture Change
Redesign your organisation and focus on customer and employee needs, training, empowerment and innovation

Death Strategies
If there is no growth and you do nothing, your organisation will die

11

STEP 4   Corporate Tactics

Tactical planning is an important part of the strategic planning process and management consultants are often asked to assist in preparing tactical plans. Tactics are the specific actions necessary to get results from all functions within the organisation, including sales, production, finance, HR, distribution and marketing.

This means that your marketing plan is a corporate tactic.

CORPORATE TACTICS					
SALES	MARKETING	PRODUCTION	FINANCIAL	HR	DISTRIBUTION
Objectives & Strategies	Objectives & Strategies	Objectives & Strategies	Objectives & Strategies	Objectives & Strategies	Objectives & Strategies
SALES PLAN	MARKETING PLAN	PRODUCTION PLAN	FINANCIAL PLAN	HR PLAN	DISTRIBUTION PLAN

2. MARKETING PLANNING

Introduction

Creating a successful marketing plan is essential to the success of your business, especially in the current economic environment. A great marketing plan will accelerate business growth, help you to acquire and retain customers and increase your market share. Great planning is the key, because if you fail to plan, you plan to fail.

This chapter provides an overview of the marketing plan to help you to understand the continuous planning process, which you will need to update regularly as the business environment changes. There will be more details on each stage in the following chapters. So, before you start marketing planning, you need to understand marketing.

What is Marketing?

MARKETING IS...

... the management process, which identifies, anticipates and satisfies customer needs and profitably.
(The Chartered Institute of marketing CIM)

Marketing is in the mind – yours and the minds of your customers.

What is a Marketing Plan?

A MARKETING PLAN IS...

... a plan for the systematic application of marketing resources to achieve your marketing objectives. It works by assessing resources and competencies, identifying market opportunities, developing objectives, strategies and tactics, implementing your marketing plan, evaluation, control and contingency planning.

What is a Ninja Marketing Plan?

A NINJA MARKETING PLAN IS...

... the same as a marketing plan, but faster, more flexible and cost effective, more dynamic, proactive and targeted, better at maximising your resources and more audacious, innovative and creative.

FACTS

- Products and services can't always find customers willing or able to buy
- Customers willing or able to buy can't always find the products
  - and services they want or need
- Ninja Marketers bring customers and suppliers together
- Ninja Marketing Plans deliver, at the right time, in the right place and at the right price

Why Do You Need a Marketing Plan?

- To have clear objectives and effective strategies, tactics and action plans
- To maximise results from your allocated resources
- To focus, integrate and coordinate all marketing activities
- To help you make informed and effective decisions
- To give you the ability to anticipate and respond to changes in the environment
- To exploit opportunities in the marketplace
- To identify and reduce risks
- To ensure that your organisation will be more customer focused
- To gain and sustain competitive advantage
- To have a benchmark against which you can measure your performance

THE MARKETING PLANNING PROCESS

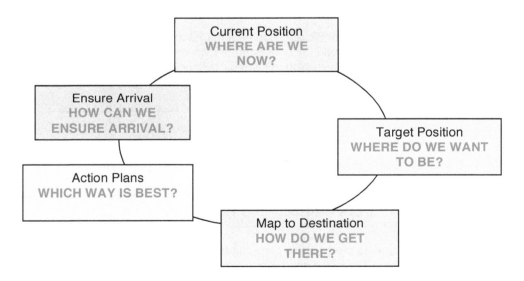

14

3. THE MARKETING PLANNING PROCESS

THE 3 STAGES OF MARKETING PLANNING		
Short-term **Annual plans**	**Medium-term** **2-5 year plans**	**Long-term** **5+ year plans**
Objectives Strategy Tactics Action plans	Objectives Strategy Tactics Action plans	Objectives Strategy Tactics Action plans
Operational planning		**Strategic planning**
Your strategy and action plans should work together		

STEP 1   Define Your Current Position

Internal Marketing Audit to Identify Your Strengths and Weaknesses
Start by identifying your target markets, your customers and the influences on their buying behavior. Identify and analyse your competitors. Analyse your resources, including the 5Ms: money, manpower, machinery, materials and marketing. Use your internal records such as databases and employee surveys.

External Marketing Audit to Identify External Opportunities and Threats
Carry out market research to monitor trends and changes in the external business environment. Use existing in-house (secondary) sources first and then you can commission external (primary) sources if necessary.

STEP 2   Evaluate Risks and Opportunities – The SWOT Analysis
Draw up a SWOT analysis to analyse the results of your market research. Classify the information by internal strengths and weaknesses and external opportunities and threats.

STEP 3   Formulate Your Marketing Objectives
The results of your SWOT analysis form the basis of your marketing objectives, which will help achieve your corporate objectives and develop your marketing plan. Commitment to your objectives is the key to successful planning, so you need to decide what you want to achieve, have a clear statement of where you want to be in marketing terms, formulate short, medium and long-term objectives that are SMART (Specific, Measurable, Achievable, Realistic and Time specific) and review your objectives regularly.

STEP 4   Plan Your Marketing Strategies
Your marketing planning strategies are the means by which you will achieve your marketing objectives and plan your tactics. Plan your strategies using gap analysis to identify the gaps between your target and actual performance and plan strategies to fill those gaps.

STEP 5 **Target Your Markets**
Identify your target markets and then profile each one using variables, including demographic profiles, buying behaviour, industry, position, needs and values. Position your organisation in their minds as their first choice by promoting its benefits and developing a strong brand proposition.

STEP 6 **Plan Your Tactics**
Plan your marketing tactics to implement your strategies by making efficient use of your resources and identifying the Critical Success Factors (CSFs).

STEP 7 **Plan Your Budget and Timelines**
Determine the cost of implementing each stage of your marketing plan over a defined period (usually your company's financial year). You should provide a contingency fund to cover unforeseen events and plot the phases of your marketing activities and the matching expenditure on a Gantt chart.

STEP 8 **Plan Your Evaluation and Control**
Compare your actual performance against your targets to identify any gaps and then plan strategies to fill those gaps.

STEP 9 **Prepare Contingency Plans**
Prepare your contingency plans in advance and review and test them regularly.

4. THE MARKETING PLAN

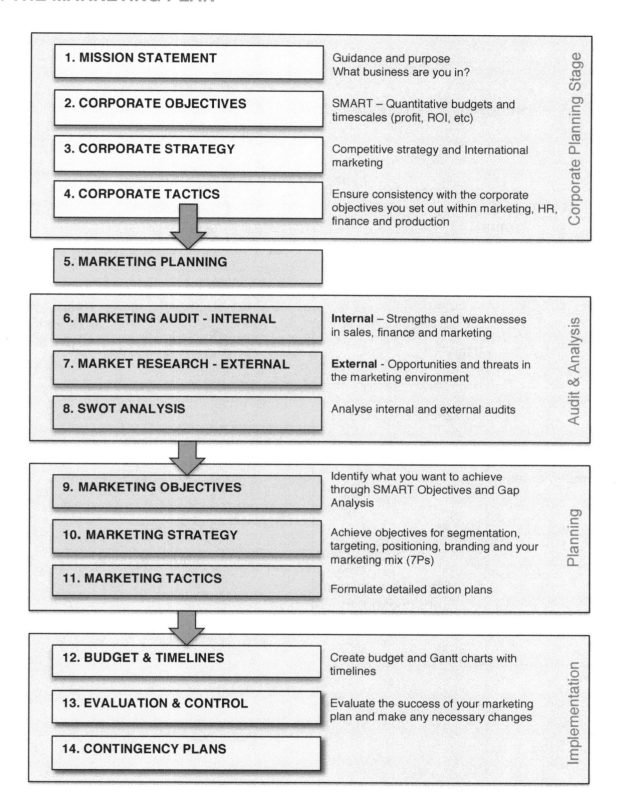

1. MISSION STATEMENT — Guidance and purpose. What business are you in?

2. CORPORATE OBJECTIVES — SMART – Quantitative budgets and timescales (profit, ROI, etc)

3. CORPORATE STRATEGY — Competitive strategy and International marketing

4. CORPORATE TACTICS — Ensure consistency with the corporate objectives you set out within marketing, HR, finance and production

Corporate Planning Stage

5. MARKETING PLANNING

6. MARKETING AUDIT - INTERNAL — **Internal** – Strengths and weaknesses in sales, finance and marketing

7. MARKET RESEARCH - EXTERNAL — **External** - Opportunities and threats in the marketing environment

8. SWOT ANALYSIS — Analyse internal and external audits

Audit & Analysis

9. MARKETING OBJECTIVES — Identify what you want to achieve through SMART Objectives and Gap Analysis

10. MARKETING STRATEGY — Achieve objectives for segmentation, targeting, positioning, branding and your marketing mix (7Ps)

11. MARKETING TACTICS — Formulate detailed action plans

Planning

12. BUDGET & TIMELINES — Create budget and Gantt charts with timelines

13. EVALUATION & CONTROL — Evaluate the success of your marketing plan and make any necessary changes

14. CONTINGENCY PLANS

Implementation

5. MARKETING PLANNING TIMESCALES (Example)

Chapter 3 - THE MARKETING ENVIRONMENT

1. THE MARKETING ENVIRONMENT

Introduction

Your organisation operates within the business environment, which includes all the internal and external factors that affect the daily operation and success of your business. Some of these factors are controllable and some are not.

You need to be aware of both internal and external influences on your marketing planning. This means carrying out an internal marketing audit and external market research, the results of which will form the basis of your marketing plan. An understanding of the marketing environment in which your business operates is essential to developing a great marketing plan.

The continuous monitoring and analysis of the external forces affecting your business is vital because the marketing environment is subject to increasingly rapid change, uncertainty and disruption. This information will help you to make your marketing plan flexible, so that you can keep ahead of changing external forces.

Think of the external environment as the big picture and the context in which you will design your marketing plan. Don't let the environment limit your creativity, but allow it to influence your choices and help you make more informed decisions.

What is the Marketing Environment?

THE MARKETING ENVIRONMENT IS...
 ... the combination of all the external factors and forces that affect your ability to build and maintain a competitive advantage.

ELEMENTS OF THE ENVIRONMENT

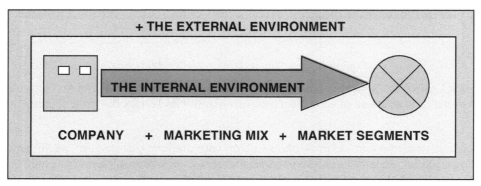

Internal	Micro	Macro
5Ms	**5Cs**	**SLEPT**
Manpower	Customers	Social
Money	Competitors	Legal
Materials	Costs	Economic
Machinery	Channels	Political
Marketing	Communication	Technological
Control	**Some Control**	**No Control**

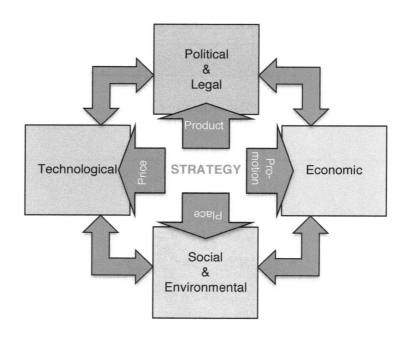

2. THE INTERNAL MARKETING ENVIRONMENT

Introduction

The internal marketing environment includes all the activities inside your organisation that affect your marketing operations. This includes all departments, such as operations, finance, human resources and management, which all have an impact on marketing decisions. The internal marketing environment also includes controllable variables such as, the marketing mix (7Ps), and the 5Ms.

7Ps	5Ms
Product	Manpower
Price	Materials
Place	Markets
Promotion	Money
People	Machinery
Process	Manpower
Physical evidence	

21

3. THE EXTERNAL MARKETING ENVIRONMENT

Introduction

The external marketing environment is made up of the uncontrollable forces outside of your organisation that can impact on your business. Although you have no control over these forces, you can respond and formulate effective strategies to adapt your business. You can turn threats into opportunities by using controllable factors from within your internal marketing environment, such as your marketing mix.

Main Factors In The External Marketing Environment	
Political	Trade agreements
	Treaties
	Political trends, including policies and taxes
	Government regimes
Economic	Economic conditions – recession or growth
	Markets
	Income and employment levels
	Inflation and interest rate
	Exchange rates
Social	Values and beliefs
	Diet, health and lifestyle
	Demographics
	Population changes, language and religion
	Social and cultural trends
Technological	Rate of technological change
	The Internet, mobile phones and social media
	E-commerce
Legal	Legislation
	Codes and practices
	Market regulations
Environmental	Competitors
	Energy consumption
	Pollution monitoring

Chapter 4 – THE MARKETING AUDIT

1. THE INTERNAL AND EXTERNAL MARKETING AUDITS

Introduction

The marketing audit, both internal and external helps you analyse and evaluate your organisation's marketing objectives, strategies, tactics, activities and results. The process takes time, but is essential to your marketing plan. The marketing audit should focus on communicating a consistent message to the right customers, reveal new markets, and help adapt your current strategies to increase your market share.

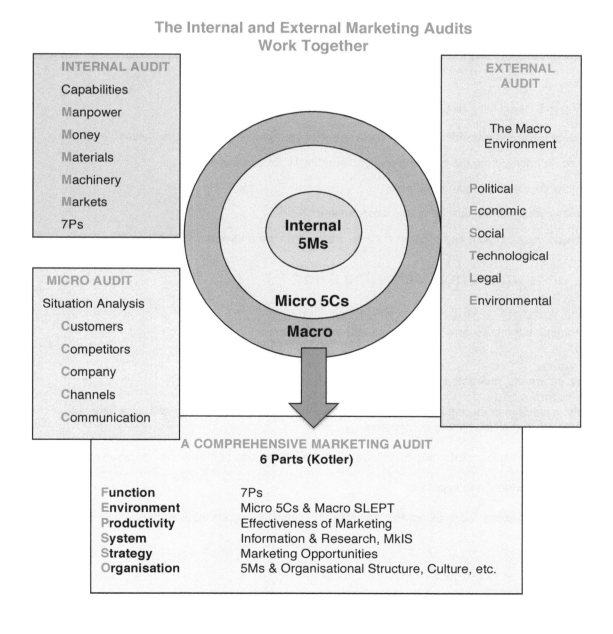

The Internal and External Marketing Audits Work Together

INTERNAL AUDIT
- Capabilities
- Manpower
- Money
- Materials
- Machinery
- Markets
- 7Ps

MICRO AUDIT
- Situation Analysis
  - Customers
  - Competitors
  - Company
  - Channels
  - Communication

Internal
5Ms

Micro 5Cs

Macro

EXTERNAL AUDIT

The Macro Environment

- Political
- Economic
- Social
- Technological
- Legal
- Environmental

A COMPREHENSIVE MARKETING AUDIT
6 Parts (Kotler)

Function	7Ps
Environment	Micro 5Cs & Macro SLEPT
Productivity	Effectiveness of Marketing
System	Information & Research, MkIS
Strategy	Marketing Opportunities
Organisation	5Ms & Organisational Structure, Culture, etc.

2. THE INTERNAL MARKETING AUDIT

Introduction

Let's start with the internal marketing audit. This is an audit to evaluate the effectiveness of your existing marketing activities. The internal marketing audit should include your Unique Selling Propositions (USPs), your strengths, your weaknesses and areas that need improvement in your existing skills and resources.

What is an Internal Marketing Audit?

AN INTERNAL MARKETING AUDIT IS...
… a systematic, critical and impartial appraisal of your existing marketing activities to identify strengths and weaknesses and to highlight any areas that need improvement.

Why Do You Need an Internal Marketing Audit?

- To have a clear understanding of the effectiveness of your current marketing activities
- To keep on track during the planning and implementation of your marketing plan
- To review your existing marketing plan
- To identify your internal strengths and weaknesses
- To provide value, insight and recommendations based on the analysis and assessment of data

Elements of Your Internal Marketing Audit

Situation Analysis – Micro Audit 5Cs
Look at the situation, the impact on your business and your options

Customers
Needs, segments, characteristics, demographics and buying behaviour
Competitors
Identify, assess their strategies and tactics, market share, products and services, strengths and weaknesses and predict future competitors
Company
Goals, market position, performance, efficiency and effectiveness of marketing operations
Channels
Distribution channels and suppliers
Communication
Your target audiences, advertising, PR, social media, website, mobile website and mobile applications (apps)

Internal Capabilities Audit (5Ms)
Look at the situation, the impact on your business and your options

Manpower
Your staff, their roles, responsibilities and effectiveness
Money
Budgets and constraints
Materials
Stock, distribution, logistics and suppliers
Machinery
Equipment and computer hardware
Markets
Your markets, market share, customer loyalty, opportunities, threats and risks

The Effectiveness of Your Marketing Mix (7Ps)
Look at where you are now, where you want to be and the gaps

Product
Your products, their market share and their competitors
Price
Your pricing policies, discounts and comparison with competitors
Place
Distribution
Promotion
Your promotional activities and their effectiveness
People
Staff, stakeholders, quality of recruitment and training
Processes
Procedures and their effectiveness
Physical Evidence
Corporate identity and promotions, including your logo, strapline, website, social media, printed material and the impressions they create

Unique Selling Propositions (USPs) Audit

THE PROCESS

STEP 1   **Research Customers and their Values**
Research how customers in your market segments make buying decisions and what your customers value about your products and services and those of your competitors.

STEP 2   **Analyse Your Research**
Analysing your research will improve your understanding of your USPs. In addition to the results of your market research, analyse feedback from your sales and customer services teams and most importantly, from your customers.

STEP 3   **Score Yourself and Your Competitors by USPs**
Identify your top competitors. Score yourself and each of your competitors out of 10 for each USP. Base your scores on objective data and look at USPs from a customer's perspective.

STEP 4   **Rank Yourself and Your Competitors by USPs**
Plot these points on a competitor analysis graph to identify your competitors' strengths and weaknesses compared to yours.

STEP 5   **Write a Simple Statement of Your USPs**
Write a statement describing your USPs and how they benefit your customers

TIPS
<ul><li>Identify your USPs and make sure that they really matter to potential customers</li><li>There's point in being the best at something that isn't important to the customers in your target markets</li><li>Preserve your USPs and use them</li><li>Defend your USPs against your competitors</li><li>Keep improving to stay ahead of your competitors</li><li>Once you've established a USP, make sure your target markets know about it</li></ul>

YOUR USP ANALYSIS

Score 1-10, 1= poor, 5 = good, 10 = excellent

USP	YOU	COMPETITOR 1	COMPETITOR 2	COMPETITOR 3

Competitor Analysis

Score out of 10							
10							
8							
6							
4							
2							
0							

USPs

Your USP Statement

3. THE EXTERNAL MARKETING AUDIT

Introduction

Your business does not operate in isolation - it's affected by your customers and your competitors and uncontrollable external forces affect you all. The external marketing audit is an audit of the external forces that affect your organisation. You need to consider all the areas of the external environment and how any changes will impact on your business, your marketing strategies and your competitors.

The external audit should look at the competitive environment, including your competitors, new entrants to the market, substitute products and services and suppliers.

Use a PESTLE analysis to identify the external forces affecting your organisation. These include political, economic. social, technological, legal and environmental forces.

What is an External Marketing Audit?

AN EXTERNAL MARKETING AUDIT IS ...
... a systematic approach to gather information about the external environment, which is necessary for your organisation to identify key issues

Why Do You Need an External Marketing Audit?

- To identify opportunities and threats, future events and trends that may impact your organisation
- To understand your competitive marketing position
- To identify which markets, products and services will provide opportunities in the future
- To be aware of threats in the environment so that they can be overcome or avoided
- To understand your internal strengths and weaknesses and to focus on your strengths to overcome your weaknesses or convert them into strengths
- To understand your competitors, minimise threats and exploit opportunities in the external environment
- To formulate a marketing plan to improve your marketing performance and gain a sustainable competitive advantage

.

YOUR EXTERNAL MARKETING AUDIT

PESTLE Audit

FACTOR	WHAT'S HAPPENING	IMPACT	OPTIONS
Political			
Economic			
Social			
Technological			
Legal			
Environmental			

Porter's 5 Forces Audit

FORCE	WHAT'S HAPPENING	IMPACT	OPTIONS
Competitive rivalry			
Bargaining power of customers			
Bargaining power of suppliers			
Threat of new entrants			
Threat of substitute products and services			

Chapter 5 – ANALYSIS

1. THE SWOT ANALYSIS

The SWOT Analysis is a great way of understanding your strengths and weaknesses and the opportunities and threats in the business environment. It was created by Albert S. Humphrey in the 1960s. It's a highly effective method for summarising your current marketing situation and analysing the results of your marketing audit. It's a framework that will help you identify any areas that may need your attention. A SWOT Analysis will help you gain a sustainable competitive advantage in your chosen market segments.

What Is a SWOT Analysis?

A SWOT ANALYSIS IS ...
… a simple, useful framework for analysing your internal strengths and weaknesses and the external opportunities and threats in the business environment.

Why Do You Need a SWOT Analysis?

- So that you can understand your internal strengths and weaknesses and focus on your strengths and overcome your weaknesses or convert them to strengths

- It enables you to understand your competitors, minimise threats and exploit opportunities in the external environment

- You can use the SWOT analysis for strategy formulation or as a strategy tool to differentiate yourself from your competitors and gain a sustainable competitive advantage.

Internal Marketing Analysis

- Your strengths, which you should exploit

- Your weaknesses and areas which need improvement in your present skills and resources

- Convert weaknesses to strengths

External Marketing Analysis

- Opportunities in the environment, which you should exploit

- Threats in the environment, which you should convert to opportunities

- Identify your strengths which can be used to exploit opportunities

- Your SWOT analysis is the starting point for strategy formulation
- Only use precise, not vague information
- Look at the most significant factors and prioritise them
- Use the options generated in your strategy formulation
- Apply in the appropriate areas of the marketing mix
- Use in conjunction with other strategy tools

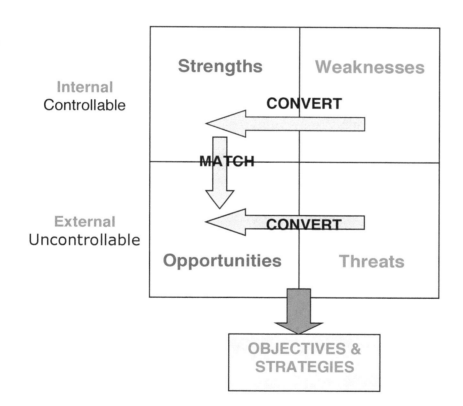

THE SWOT ANALYSIS PROCESS

STEP 1   **Analyse Your Strengths**
Examine your strengths from an internal perspective
Identify what you do better than your competitors
Find out what the customers in your market perceive as your strengths
Look at what differentiates you from your competitors
Focus on your Unique Selling Propositions (USPs) and what you do better than your competitors

STEP 2   **Analyse Your Weaknesses**
Identify any weaknesses that could threaten your business
Find weaknesses that can be converted into strengths
Research how customers in your target market perceive your weaknesses
Identify the reasons you lose customers
Be realistic and objective

STEP 3   **Find Your Opportunities**
Identify any strengths that can be used to create opportunities
Look for trends in the environment
Find opportunities created by changes in the external environment, including technology, markets, government policy, legislation, social patterns, population profiles and lifestyles
Identify local and international opportunities

STEP 4   **Identify Threats**
Identify any competitive threats
Monitor changes in quality standards or specifications for your products and services
Track changes in the external business environment, including political, legal, regulatory, economic, sociological and technological developments
Identify any factors in the environment that could threaten your business

YOUR SWOT ANALYSIS

YOUR STRENGTHS

What you do well
Your USPs
What others see as your strengths

YOUR WEAKNESSES

What you could improve
Resources you might need
What others see as your weaknesses

OPPORTUNITIES

Your opportunities
Trends you could exploit
Turn your strengths into opportunities

EXTERNAL THREATS

Threats to your business
Your competition
Threats caused by your weaknesses

2. MARKET RESEARCH

Introduction

Market research is a vital part of marketing planning because markets worldwide are highly competitive. It's an essential tool for planning your objectives and strategies to achieve the best results.

Market research should be done continually, to keep up with market trends, to understand your target markets and to maintain your competitive edge. It starts with the collection of data and necessary marketing information, from secondary research (desk research) and primary research (commissioned research). It enables you to make informed decisions by increasing your understanding of your internal and external marketing environment.

What is Market Research?

MARKET RESEARCH IS...
... the process of gathering, analysing and interpreting information about a market, its products and services, existing and potential customers, their characteristics, spending habits, location and needs.

Why Use Market Research?

Know Your Markets

- To obtain current and accurate information on the external environment

- To obtain information about your position in the market, your market share, it's size and market trends

- To understand the competition, their products and services and to anticipate competitive moves

- To gain insight into key trends and behaviour in your markets

- To enable you to make informed decisions

- To guide future innovation

Know Your Customers (KYC)

- To identify and understand your customers, their needs and expectations and how they change over time

- To cross sell and upsell in order to increase business from your existing customers

- To understand the value of each customer, to identify which customers are at risk and why customers are lost

THE MARKET RESEARCH PROCESS

STEP 1   **Secondary Research**
Use research from existing sources first because it's quicker, easier and cheaper. These sources include your internal databases, the internet, social media, published information and surveys.

STEP 2   **Primary Research**
Use specially commissioned research, which is designed for your specific purpose, to get information that is not available from secondary research. This can be time consuming and expensive.

SOURCES OF INFORMATION

Contact Information

- Information, recommendations and referrals from customers
- Enquiries
- Leads from telemarketers and your sales force
- Promotions and competitions
- List brokers who can be hired or lists bought from commercial brokers
- Your customer database

Customer Information

- Electronic Point Of Sale (EPOS)
- Your database and transaction documents
- Customer feedback, focus groups, interviews and group discussions
- Coupons, entry forms, prize draws, competitions, etc.
- Exhibitions and conferences
- Direct observation, by studying customers and what, when and how much they buy
- Sales force information, because they know your customers best
- Customer Surveys, to get their opinions, ideas and suggestions on satisfaction, price and service
- Customer loyalty programmes, which combine customer care and marketing research

3. THE MARKETING DATABASE

Introduction

A marketing database usually contains contact, personal and transaction details from internal marketing, sales or delivery systems. It can also contain lists purchased from organisations that have collected this information. Marketing databases have a variety of uses, from market research, cross selling, upselling and contacting prospective customers and suppliers to customer acquisition and retention.

There are two main types of marketing database: customer databases and business databases. Customer databases contain simple customer information, whilst business databases are more complicated and comprehensive. Use your database to organise your data so that it's easy to track and that the same accurate, current data and information is available to everyone in your organisation who needs it.

What is a Database?

A DATABASE IS...
...a system for the storage, retrieval and use of data and information, which is centrally stored and shared by all users.

Why Do You Need a Database?

- To avoid duplication of data in files held by different users
- To avoid inconsistency in the organisation's customer and marketing data
- To ensure the integrity of your customer and marketing data and information
- To identify your most profitable customers, trends in the market and opportunities and threats
- To facilitate market research, data processing direct mail, sales, transactional processing, planning and product development and improvement

TYPES OF MARKETING DATABASES

Flat Files

- All data is stored in a single table database like the telephone directory
- Easy to build and maintain
- OK for simple applications like mailing lists

Relational Database

- Splits up the data into tables, which can be linked and integrated
- Can produce reports and lists
- Greater flexibility
- Better storage and retrieval

Database Maintenance and Updates

- Systematically and regularly maintain and update your database
- Record all inbound and outbound contact
- Record contacts and customers
- Transfer contacts and prospects who become customers to customer database and delete from contacts and prospects database
- Add additional information, new names and records to your database
- Add new fields to accommodate new information
- Record feedback from contacts and customers
- Delete customer or prospect details from your database if requested

4. MARKETING ANALYTICS

Introduction

Marketing analytics are the methods used to analyse data. These methods enable you to obtain information on customer needs, the features and solutions they're looking for in products and services, changes in their behavior or preferences and the activities of your competitors.

What is Marketing Analytics?

MARKETING ANALYTICS IS...
... the practice of measuring, managing and analysing marketing data and turning it into information that can be used to formulate your marketing plan.

Analytic System

TYPES OF ANALYTIC SYSTEMS	
Transaction Processing Systems	• Routine handling of data and transactions
Management Information Systems (MkiS)	• Information for managers • There are 3 levels of management information: strategic, tactical and operational • The best system for marketing research
Executive Information Systems	• Strategic level information • Key internal and external data • Identifies problems rather than solves them
Decision Support Systems	• Not very user friendly • Used by middle managers for routine modeling • Solve issues which are unstructured • Analyses problems for senior executives
Expert Systems	• Computer programs containing expert knowledge, information and advice • Specialised data, including legal, engineering, etc • Used at operational level for structured problems

5. MARKETING INFORMATION SYSTEM – MkiS

Introduction

Marketing information systems analyse data and provide information to be used as a basis for strategic marketing planning. They help you to make informed decisions in planning and implementing your marketing plan. A Marketing Information System (MkIS) has 4 parts:

- The internal reports system which includes orders, inventories and invoices
- The marketing research system stores research, both continuous and ad hoc
- The marketing intelligence system is used by managers and is less specific
- The analytical marketing system interprets data and information from market research

What Is a Marketing Information System?

A MARKETING INFORMATION SYSTEM (MkiS) IS...
… all computer and non-computer systems that collect, analyse, store and communicate relevant data and information.

Why Do You Need a Marketing Information System?

- To monitor the business environment
- To analyse data from internal audits and external research
- To determine customer attitudes
- To monitor your competitors
- To segment and target your markets
- To measure performance
- To monitor and control your timelines and budgets
- To evaluate alternative strategies
- To co-ordinate your marketing and sales planning and implementation

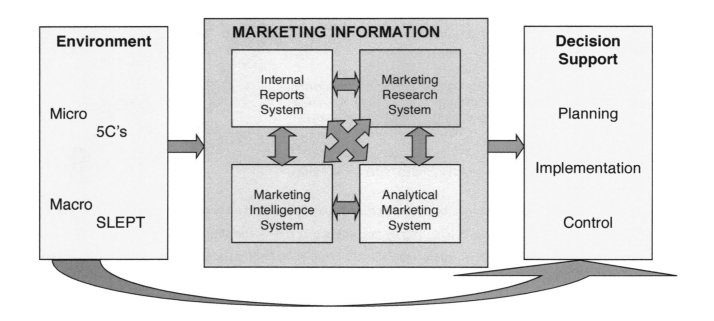

COMPONENTS OF THE MkiS	
INTERNAL REPORTING SYSTEM • Company records • Results data • Strengths & weaknesses • Sales, costs, stock, etc.	**MARKETING RESEARCH SYSTEM** • Specific purpose • Marketing problems • Opportunities and threats • Effectiveness
ANALYTICAL MARKETING SYSTEM • Computerised modeling software • Decision support • Models to explain and predict scenarios • Simulation – 'What If' scenarios	**MARKETING INTELLIGENCE SYSTEM** • Ongoing monitoring of the environment • Monitors changes in the environment • General, Micro, Macro

THE COMPUTERISED MkiS

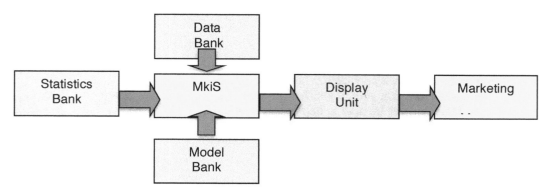

COMPONENTS OF THE COMPUTERISED MkiS	
DATA BANK • Stores marketing data from marketing research findings	**STATISTICAL BANK** • Stores programs for computing sales forecasts • Stores advertising spend projections, calculating productivity, etc.
MODEL BANK • Stores marketing models for planning and analysis	**DISPLAY UNIT** • VDU screen and keyboard • Marketing reports can be viewed, o e-mailed and printed

Chapter 6 - MARKETING OBJECTIVES

1. MARKETING OBJECTIVES

Introduction

Marketing objectives define what you want to accomplish through your marketing activities. When developing your specific marketing objectives, it's important to be realistic and ensure that your objectives are achievable in a specified time period and that you will be able to demonstrate whether or not they were achieved. Clear marketing objectives enable you to formulate the appropriate marketing strategies to achieve your marketing objectives.

What is an Objective?

A MARKETING OBJECTIVE IS...
 ... a specific marketing result that you want to achieve with defined resources, within a stated time frame to predetermined standards.

SMART Objectives

Specific
Measurable
Achievable
Realistic
Time specific

2. THE DIFFERENCE BETWEEN CORPORATE OBJECTIVES AND MARKETING OBJECTIVES

Corporate Objectives

Corporate objectives are expressed in terms of a financial outcome that is to be achieved by the organisation as a whole. Some examples are: turnover, profit, return on investment (ROI), sales volumes, growth, value of the business and dividend paid to shareholders.

Marketing Objectives

Marketing strategies and tactics are designed to achieve both corporate and marketing objectives. Corporate objectives, marketing objectives, marketing strategies and marketing tactics can be expressed as a hierarchy (the marketing plan).

Some examples of marketing objectives:

- To maintain or increase market share by 20% in the next year

- To innovate and create, develop and launch 10 new products in the next 5 years

- To enter 5 new markets by the end of next year

- To change market positioning to become number one in the market in the next 2 years

EXAMPLES OF CORPORATE AND MARKETING OBJECTIVES

Corporate Objective
To grow profits by 20% each year for the next 5 years

Marketing Objective
To increase UK market share by 50% in the next year

43

3. MARKET SEGMENTATION

Introduction

Market segmentation is the process of dividing the market into groups of existing or potential customers with similar characteristics, needs or buying behavior. You can then target the segment or segments that you want to address and position your products and services in their minds relative to your competitors. The next step is to develop a strong brand that differentiates you from your competitors and makes you their first choice.

Your marketing will be more effective if you can group, categorise and target your customers according to identifiable characteristics or variables. This enables you to formulate an effective marketing strategy for each of your chosen market segments. The process of market segmentation, targeting, positioning and branding is fundamental in understanding marketing and marketing strategy. The objectives of market segmentation are to improve your company's competitive position and better satisfy the needs of your customers. Some specific objectives may include improved market share and enhanced brand image. Before we go on to market segmentation, we need to define a market.

What is a Market?

A MARKET IS...
... a group of individuals, groups or organisations with a common need and who:  <ul><li>need or want your products and services</li><li>are willing to use their buying power</li><li>have the ability to purchase</li><li>have the authority to purchase</li></ul>

What is Segmentation?

SEGMENTATION IS...
... dividing a market into segments of people or organisations that have something in common, for example: age, social class, spending power, gender or buying behavior. An effective market segment is: **M**easurable, **A**ccessible, **S**ubstantial and **S**ustainable.

Why Segment Your Markets?

- To ensure that you target the right market segments
- To design a specific marketing mix for each segment
- To make it easier to identify your prospective customers
- To estimate the size of your markets and identify any gaps in the market
- To understand your competitors and position your brand in relation to theirs
- To ensure that your products and services will satisfy customer needs and wants
- To gain a better understanding of your customers enabling more customer focus
- To respond quickly to any changes in the market
- To budget more effectively
- To target segments that are easier and more cost effective to enter and maintain

SEGMENTATION IS A BALANCING ACT

For effective segmentation, you need to achieve a balance between your resources and objectives. If you don't have enough resources, change your objectives.

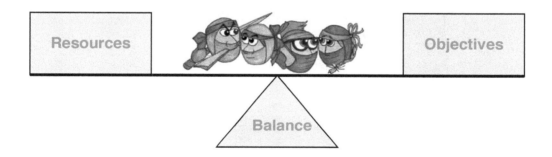

How Much Segmentation?

To effectively target your market segments, you need to find the right balance for your business and resources between two extremes. Weigh the costs against the benefits of tighter segmentation, when you reach a balance – STOP!

ACHIEVE THE RIGHT BALANCE

Achieve balance between the two extremes, one product for the entire world and one product for each person:

- Choose your own niche in markets where you can become a leader
- Use segmentation variables, such as: buying behaviour, common needs, preferences and characteristics, be creative and think outside the box
- Divide the total market into segments
- Choose the segments you want to address
- Then target each market with a unique marketing mix

SEGMENTATION STRATEGY

Customer characteristics, buying behaviour or needs

↓

MARKET SEGMENTS

↓

Your capabilities should match the needs of your chosen segments

↓

TARGET YOUR MARKETS

↓

Your Marketing Mix - 7Ps
Product
Price
Place
Promotion
People
Process
Physical evidence

EXAMPLE: SEGEMENTING THE CAR MARKET

Car market segmented by customer needs
Cost, pleasure, comfort, reliability, image, safety, speed, service

Your company's capabilities must match your segment's and customer needs

7Ps =the marketing mix
Product, **P**rice, **P**lace, **P**romotion, **P**eople, **P**rocess, **P**hysical evidence
Aim a separate marketing mix at each segment

SATISFYING NEEDS OF EACH SEGMENT IN THE CAR MARKET

THE NEED FOR TRANSPORT
Needs remain constant, ways of satisfying them change

OLD

NEW

Cost	Pleasure	Comfort	Reliability	Image	Safety	Speed	Service
Skoda	BMW	Rolls Royce	Toyota	Ferrari	Volvo	Aston Martin	Hyundai

CUSTOMERS SEGMENTED BY NEEDS
SATISFY THE NEEDS OF EACH SEGMENT

THE MARKET SEGMENTATION PROCESS

STEP 1   **Define Each of Your Markets**

Use available surveys and information to clearly define your target markets. Sort them into smaller groups that have similar characteristics or behaviour, to get segments that you can enter and defend against competitors.

STEP 2   **Segment Each Market**

Be creative in using segmentation variables to identify customers with similar characteristics or behaviour in order to construct your segments.

SEGMENTATION VARIABLES	
Demographic	Measurable characteristics, such as age, occupation, etc
Socio-economic	Social and economic profiles
Geographic	Country, region, city, or any geographical area
Psychographic	Lifestyle, attitude, values, activities, interests, opinions, etc.
Buying Behaviour	Benefits sought, usage, purchase occasions, attitude to products and services
Family Life Cycle	Situation and lifestyle changes, including income, expenditure and saving
Brand loyalty	Heavy or light users, brand loyalty or brand switchers

STEP 3   **Evaluate Your Segments**

Assess your chosen market segments to ensure that they are useable, approachable and large enough to be viable.

STEP 4   **Profile Your Segments**

Research detailed descriptions of customers in your target segments, including their needs, buying behavior, preferences, demographics or other segmentation variables.

STEP 5   **Evaluate the Attractiveness of Each Segment**

Add market data and consumer research to your segment profiles, including size, growth rates, price sensitivity and brand loyalty. Evaluate each segment for its attractiveness using a method that will produce numerical and qualitative data for each segment.

STEP 6   **Target Your Markets**

Decide which segments to target. Consider factors, including your strategy, the segment's attractiveness, barriers to entry and competitive rivalry.

STEP 7   **Position Yourself in the Minds of Your Target Markets**

Position your products and services in the minds of customers in your target segments as innovative, unique, superior or great value compared to those of your competitors.

STEP 8   **Develop and Implement a Marketing Mix**

Develop a marketing mix that will support your positioning in each of your target segments which will include an effective programme of marketing communications.

STEP 9   **Evaluate Your Performance**

Regularly evaluate your performance in each of your segments to keep on track, keep up with changes in the market and to find new opportunities.

4. TARGETING

Introduction

After dividing your markets into segments, or groups with similar characteristics, by carrying out market research and analysis, you will need to choose your target segments. One strategy and marketing mix will not be appropriate for all your target segments. The next step is to develop a specific strategy and marketing mix for each segment.

The marketing mix of product, price, place, promotion, people, process and physical evidence (the 7Ps) are the elements of targeting strategy that will determine your success in your target market segments. A well-defined target segment is the first element to a successful marketing strategy.

What is Targeting?

TARGETING IS...
… the identification and measurement of target market segments in order to make informed decisions about which group to target and aim a different marketing mix at each segment.

Why Do You Need to Target Your Segments?

- To maximise your marketing budget
- To formulate a marketing strategy and marketing mix for each segment
- To better satisfy customer needs

THE TARGETING PROCESS

STEP 1   **Identify Your Target Market Segments**
Using available surveys and information, clearly define your target segments and identify and sort them into groups that have similar characteristics or behaviour to get market segments that you can enter, maintain and defend against competitors.

STEP 2   **Segment Your Market**
Your next step is to segment the market. Be creative in using segmentation variables to identify customers in your target markets.

STEP 3   **Design a Specific Marketing Mix for Each Segment**
Make a big impact using a specifically designed marketing mix, including product, price, place, promotion and the elements of customer service: people, process and physical evidence.

TIPS
WHEN TARGETING A NEW MARKET
DON'T FORGET TO DEFEND YOUR EXISTING MARKETS AGAINST THE ENEMY
SHOOT IN A TARGET RICH ENVIRONMENT!!!   TARGET YOUR MARKET SEGMENTS

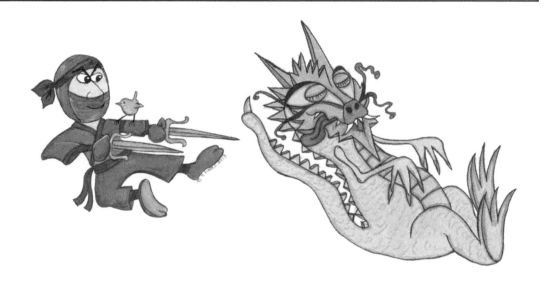

5. POSITIONING

Introduction

Market positioning is the process used to influence your customers' perceptions of your brand, products and services in relation to those of your competitors.

To achieve your positioning objectives, you need to understand how your competitors position themselves, the benefits sought by your target market segments and you must identify which of your USPs will satisfy their needs better than the competition.

Positioning is one of the most important factors in formulating your marketing strategies. You will be positioned in the market even if you do nothing, however, you can influence these perceptions by carefully targeting each segment with their own marketing mix. The key elements are price, quality and benefits.

What is Positioning?

POSITIONING IS...

… the process of positioning your products and services in the minds of customers in your target market segments, relative to your competitors.

Why Do You Need to Position Yourself?

- To influence customers' buying decisions
- So that customers see you as the best and first choice
- Because positioning is the basis for building a strong brand

Positioning Objectives

Value Positioning

The objective of value positioning is to price your products and services at or below market averages to attract customers who are price sensitive. You can target low to middle income customers or appeal to those who are cost conscious. Value positioning works well during a recession, a slow economic period or for a late entrant into a market.

Quality Positioning

The objective of quality positioning is to offer the highest quality products and services. Quality leaders can charge higher prices.

Demographic Positioning

The objective of demographic positioning is to use demographics, such as age and gender in order to target these market segments with a specific marketing mix that satisfies the needs of each segment.

Competitive Positioning

The objective of competitive positioning is to place your company in the minds of your target segments as being better than the competition. Comparative advertising can demonstrate that your products and services are superior.

THE POSITIONING PROCESS

STEP 1   **Know Your Target Market**

Identify your target markets. Understand their needs and preferences and know what they expect. Design a marketing mix that satisfies those needs.

STEP 2   **Identify Features of Your Products And Services**

Features and benefits are the basis of customer buying decisions and loyalty.

STEP 3   **Identify Your Unique Selling Propositions (USPs)**

Identify your USPs, ensuring that they really matter to customers in your target market segments and effectively communicate them. Invest and keep innovating to defend your USPs against your competitors.

STEP 4   **Know Your Competitors**

Be aware of your competitors' products and services. Let your target market know that your products are the best to gain competitive advantage.

STEP 5   **Your Marketing Communications**

Sell the benefits of your offerings by sending out the right message and by using the right media and effective promotional techniques.

STEP 6   **Defend and Maintain Your Position**

It's essential that you continue to live up to customers' expectations, by keeping up the quality.

Chapter 7 - BRANDING

1. BRANDING

Introduction

Your brand represents your business, your reputation, values, strengths and passions. Great brands create customer loyalty because customers identify with their favourite brands. A strong brand is one your most valuable assets. If your brand isn't strong enough, make it stronger by clearly defining what your brand stands for, its goals, personality and the brand experience that customers will receive when they come into contact with it. And you must continually deliver on that promise.

What is a Brand?

A BRAND IS ...
... a trademark or distinctive name, design or symbol, which identifies an organisation, a product or a service and distinguishes it from its competitors.

Why Do You Need a Strong and Unique Brand?

- To communicate the attributes and benefits which influence buying behaviour
- To create value
- To create brand recognition and loyalty
- To give your products and services a distinct personality
- To enhance your reputation
- To differentiate you from your competitors
- To facilitate the introduction and diffusion of new products and services
- To maximise your brand equity

TIP
Your brand should be fit to survive in the modern marketing environment and aligned with the needs and culture of your business. The most famous and long-lasting brands are the result of constant reinforcement and promotion.

THE BRANDING PROCESS

STEP 1   **Create Your Brand Positioning Statement**

Write a short statement that clearly defines the USPs and value of your products and services, which market segments they target, how they benefit your customers, how they are differentiated from your competitors and the categories in which your brand exists.

STEP 2   **Define Your Brand**

Describe what your brand offers and why, how it's different and better, what customer benefits it offers and how it will satisfy customer needs. Define your brand's core values.

STEP 3   **Create Your Brand Image**

Your name, logo and strapline are the keys to your brand image. Your logo is your marque or symbol and the image of your brand. Your strapline is a memorable phrase that summarises the attributes of your products and services and your brand and market position. Make sure you deliver a consistent brand image.

STEP 4   **Develop Your Brand's Personality**

Brands have personalities, like people and Ninjas. Apply human characteristics to your brand; the way it looks, feels, behaves, speaks, thinks, acts, and reacts and decide whether to make it fun or serious, playful or straightforward.

STEP 5   **Create a Brand Experience**

This creates the emotions you want your customers to feel when they experience your brand. It's your heart, soul and spirit.

STEP 6   **Launch Your Brand**

Go public, unveil your name, logo, and slogan and explain how your brand matches customer profiles, satisfies their needs and creates a brand experience.

STEP 7   **Manage, Build and Protect Your Brand**

Just like people and Ninjas, your brand needs consistent care and attention to make it strong, healthy and resilient and to protect it from your competitors.

STEP 8   **Keep Your Brand Current**

Occasionally change the way you present your brand. Update your brand image to keep it relevant to the current marketing environment and to ensure that it continually meets the needs of your increasingly sophisticated markets and customers.

STEP 9   **Create a Truly Global Brand**

This will create new global markets and new opportunities for your business.

YOUR BRAND ANALYSIS	
Brand Element	**Impact on Your Business**
Your Brand Image	
Your Brand Personality	
Your Brand Associations	
YOUR BRAND DEFINITION & SUMMARY	

2. BRAND LOYALTY

Introduction

Customers who are loyal to your brand will keep repurchasing your products and services. Loyal customers are great assets because it's 12 times more expensive to find new customers than to keep existing customers happy.

What is Brand Loyalty?

BRAND LOYALTY IS ...
 ... a customer's positive attitude, behaviour and commitment to your brand.

Why Do You Need to Create Brand Loyalty?

- To maximise your brand equity
- To increase the volume and value of repeat business
- To reduce price sensitivity
- To increase the number of referrals and recommendations
- To gain and retain customers

Create and Increase Brand Loyalty

- Let your customers develop an emotional attachment to your brand
- Tailor the experience to customer needs so that they engage with your brand
- Differentiate your brand from your competitors
- Create a great experience by giving your customers added value
- Create a loyalty scheme so that your customers feel part of a club
- Present offers and promotions that get customers' attention
- Reach out to a wider audience by using social media
- Launch special offers to secure loyalty
- Mobile apps can increase sales

SEGMENTATION, TARGETING, POSITIONING, BRANDING

SEGMENTATION	SEGMENTATION VARIABLES
The process of dividing a market into segments of people or organisations that have characteristics or buying behaviour in common.	Characteristics Buying behaviour Profiles Validate
TARGETING	**IDENTIFY YOUR TARGETS**
The identification and measurement of target market segments in order to make informed decisions about which segments to target with your marketing mixes. A well-defined target segment is the first element to a successful marketing strategy.	**Measurable** Measure market potential & response to marketing strategy **Approachable** Reach segments with promotion and distribution **Substantial** Size to justify attention and profitability **Sustainable** Long-term prospect – justify time and cost of development
POSITIONING	**POSITION YOURSELF**
The position of your products and services in the minds of your customers and consumers relative to your competitors.	Research & change perceptions Position yourself Perceptual maps Find gaps in the market Marketing mix for each segment
A BRAND	**DEVELOP A STRONG BRAND**
A trademark or distinctive name, design, symbol or feature, which identifies a product, service or manufacturer, distinguishing it from others	Focus on brand assets Define your core values Communicate the benefits Deliver a consistent brand image Meet the needs of your customers Manage your brand Create a global brand

3. THE BRAND EXPERIENCE

What is a Brand Experience?

A BRAND EXPERIENCE IS ...
... the way that people perceive their experience of every contact and interaction with your brand. It can include one or more or the person's five senses.

TIP
To create a consistent brand experience, don't forget to integrate the use of all aspects of digital marketing, including social media, a mobile website and mobile applications (apps) for all mobile devices.

Why Do You Need to Create a Brand Experience?

- To offer your customers the ultimate form of customer care
- To differentiate you from your competitors
- To add value to your brand
- To create good feelings about your products and services
- To increase customer loyalty and create superior long-term business results

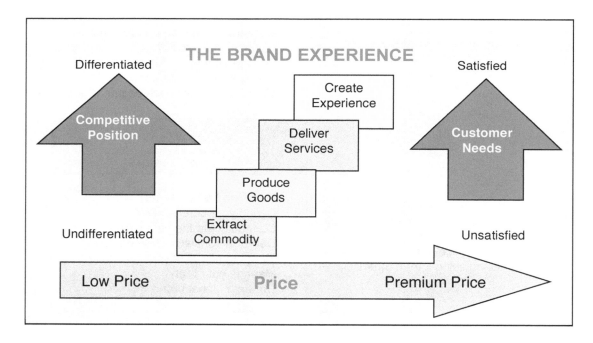

58

THE BRAND EXPERIENCE PROCESS

STEP 1   **Identify Customer Needs and Provide Solutions**

Gaining an insight into customer needs is the most vital step and lays a firm foundation for creating compelling brand experiences and greater brand loyalty. Identify customer needs, create solutions and validate them with your customers and use their feedback to refine your products and services.

STEP 2   **Promote the Benefits, Not the Features**

The value you provide to your customers is in the quality of the brand experience. Every customer is tuned in to one radio station - WIFM (what's in it for me or the WIFM factor).

STEP 3   **Understand the Context of the Experience**

One context is the environment in which the customer uses a product or service and another is who's using your products and services and their abilities or limitations. It's crucial to consider the cultural, social, emotional and physical factors that influence these contexts.

STEP 4   **Research the Whole Brand Experience**

Look at the entire brand experience, including the benefits that will lead to new opportunities and improve the overall brand experience. Consider how the customer feels and reacts before and after their experience, including how they research, buy, use and maintain your products and services, the environmental impact of your products and the range of customer interactions with your brand. Every interaction is a chance to improve the overall brand experience.

STEP 5   **Involve the Key Stakeholders**

To maximise the effectiveness of your brand experience strategy, research the requirements, motivations, aspirations, perceptions and responses to your brand, products and services. These can be gained from a range of internal and external stakeholders, including consumers, customers, opinion leaders, maintenance providers, executives, marketing, sales, engineering and supply chain management and regulatory teams.

STEP 6   **Provide Your Customers With Compelling Experiences**

Create a quality brand experience that is exciting, meaningful and engaging.

59

Chapter 8 - CUSTOMER DELIGHT

1. YOUR CUSTOMERS

Introduction

Before we tell you about customer service, loyalty and delight, it's a good idea to help you understand who your customers are and where to find them.

Who are Your Customers?

YOUR CUSTOMERS ARE...
• Existing customers • Potential customers • Customers who buy from your competitors • And worst of all – lapsed customers who have gone somewhere else

FACTS
• Customers choose products and services on the basis of perceived benefits and price • If you produce products and offer services that nobody wants, you'll soon be bankrupt

DID YOU KNOW

It's **12 times** more expensive to get a new customer
than to keep an existing customer happy

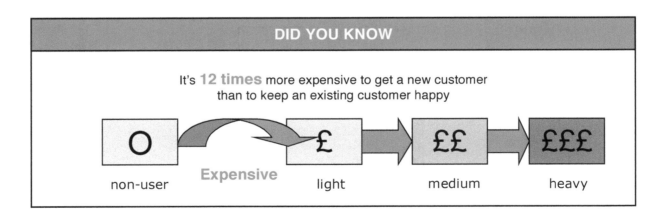

What Should You Do With Your Customers?

Existing Customers

- Keep them happy
- Sell them more of what they buy already
- Sell them new products and services

Lapsed Customers

- Get them back
- Keep them

Potential Customers

- Increase their awareness
- Find new markets
- Find new customers
- Offer products and services that meet their needs

2. CUSTOMER CARE

Introduction

A lack of customer care is a weakness of many organisations and therefore a strength that can differentiate you from your competitors. Customer care, product and service quality and good marketing result in customer loyalty. Having gained the loyalty of your existing customers, you now want to increase your market share by acquiring new markets and more customers.

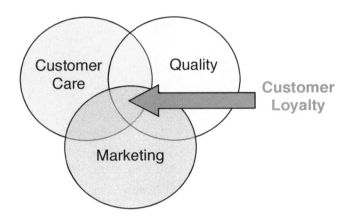

CUSTOMER CARE IS ...	
	... providing excellent customer service, before, during and after your customers make a purchase

Why Provide Great Customer Service?

- To engender customer satisfaction and loyalty
- To meet customer needs and exceed their expectations
- To gain and retain customers
- To win customer recommendations and referrals
- To generate positive customer perceptions of your company's products and services
- To increase your market share

TIP
... Don't forget to include the 3Ps of customer care in your marketing mix (7Ps) because all products contain elements of service and customer care.

THE 3Ps OF CUSTOMER CARE

People

- Employees are the people who deliver the service and their attitude, appearance, behaviour, skills and professionalism impact on your brand image, the customer experience and their perceptions about your organisation

- Customers are essential to your business, so you need to understand their values, attitudes and buying behaviour and fulfill their needs and expectations

Process

- Process is the system used to deliver customer service

- Efficiency and effectiveness in procedures saves money

- Policies are guides to decision making

- Procedures ensure that your policies are implemented

- Information sharing and effective communication are essential elements in providing excellent customer service

- Speed and accessibility of products and services help to ensure customer loyalty

Physical evidence

- Environment is where you deliver the service

- Your environment and facilities can be used to charge a premium and create a positive customer experience

- Tangible evidence includes your logo, literature, packaging and labels

3. CUSTOMER DELIGHT

Introduction

Delighted customers promote your brand and drive growth. They are loyal, buy more and encourage new customers by referrals, whilst unhappy customers could abandon your brand and may promote a negative image of your business. You should encourage and collect feedback from every customer interaction to learn about their perceptions, needs and market trends. To ensure a sustainable competitive advantage and success tomorrow, you need to delight your customers today!

What is Customer Delight?

CUSTOMER DELIGHT IS …
 … the positive response of a customer who has received a product or service that exceeds their expectations, it's receiving customer service with bells on!

Why Do You Need to Delight Your Customers

- To retain you existing customers
- To attract new customers by getting referrals and testimonials
- To let customers know that you value their business
- To make your products and services less price sensitive
- To maximise repeat business
- To increase your market share
- To enhance the value of your business

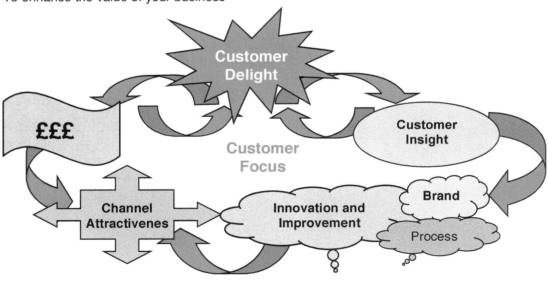

THE CUSTOMER DELIGHT PROCESS

STEP 1 **Identify Your Customers**
Identify and segment your markets into groups of customers with similar characteristics or buying behaviour.

STEP 2 **Know Your Customers**
Understand their needs and preferences, know what they expect, focus on their needs and exceed their expectations.

STEP 3 **Deliver Customer Delight**

- Exceed their expectations
- Provide an element of surprise to differentiate your business from the competition
- Innovate and think outside the box
- Deliver excellent customer service
- Listen to your customers and respond quickly to their needs
- Communicate frequently with your existing and potential customers
- Stop problems before they start
- Be better than your competition and have a positive attitude to your customers
- Integrate customer delight throughout your entire organisation

STEP 4 **Feedback**
Encourage, gather and analyse customer feedback to provide better customer care.

STEP 5 **Communicate**
Identify and share the best customer experiences and data so that everyone in your team is involved in the process.

STEP 6 **Bring Them Back**
Communicate to win back unhappy customers, keep them happy and promote customer loyalty.

STEP 7 **Analyse Your Data**
Use your data to analyse and evaluate feedback and market trends, generate new ideas and create benchmarks.

STEP 8 **Evaluate Your Performance**
Use customer feedback to focus on the issues that affect your performance and highlight any areas that need improvement.

STEP 9 **Improve Your Performance**
Improve your customer experience to delight your customers, increase market share, gain and maintain a competitive advantage and reach your marketing and corporate goals.

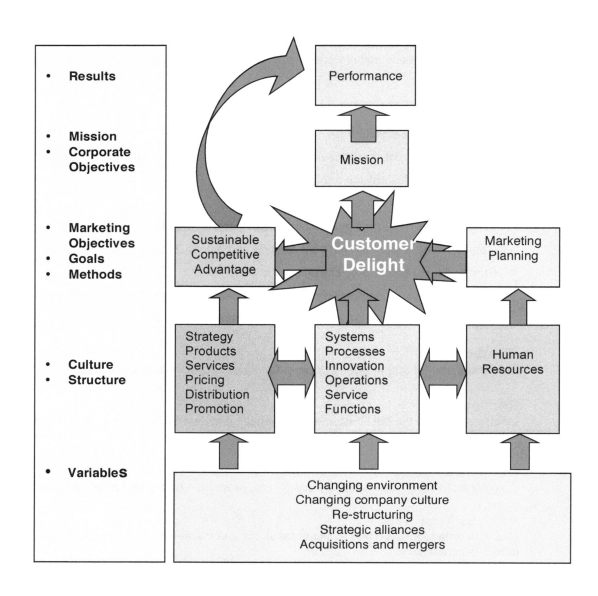

4. CUSTOMER LOYALTY PROGRAMME

Introduction

Getting and keeping customers is really difficult, especially in today's competitive environment. A customer loyalty programme is a great way to gain and retain customers. It gives them a great brand experience and engages and motivates them to buy more of your products and services. You need a creative solution where loyal customers accumulate and redeem points. This keeps your products and services in their mind as their first choice.

What is a Customer Loyalty Programme?

A CUSTOMER LOYALTY PROGRAMME IS ...
… a programme offered to loyal customers, which offers rewards, advanced access to new products, sales coupons or free merchandise.

Why Do You Need a Customer Loyalty Programme?

- To attract, acquire and retain customers
- To create customer loyalty by giving benefits and rewards
- To motivate and engage customers
- To create customer delight
- To add value to your brand
- To provide you with a wealth of information about the types of products and services purchased by your customers and the effectiveness of certain incentives

Chapter 9 - MARKETING STRATEGY

1. MARKETING STRATEGY

Introduction

Your marketing strategy is the means by which you will achieve your marketing and corporate objectives. Your marketing strategy should be divided into 1 year, 3-5 year and 5-10 year strategies. Marketing strategies are the basis for your tactical planning and your marketing action plans. Your strategy may be audacious and bold, but it's completely useless if it doesn't do the job. In other words, your marketing strategies are only good if they are implemented, delight your customers and leave your competitors at a disadvantage.

What is a Marketing Strategy?

A MARKETING STRATEGY IS...
… a process for concentrating your resources on achieving your corporate and marketing objectives.

Why Do You Need Marketing Strategies?

- To achieve your corporate and marketing objectives
- To meet the specific needs of each market segment more quickly and more effectively than your competitors
- To establish and maintain your position in the market
- To generate customer loyalty
- To focus on your strategies and your competitors' weaknesses

TIPS
• Put total customer focus and marketing orientation at the TOP of your   o agenda to win customer preference and loyalty   • Aim your strategies at the customer, not the competition, because strategies that follow the competition may impress your competitors, but not necessarily your customers   • Adjust your strategy to fit the existing marketing environment, not the other way around   • Remain flexible

2. GAP ANALYSIS

Introduction

Before you start to formulate your marketing strategies, you need to do a gap analysis to identify what needs to be done to achieve your marketing and corporate objectives. This process helps you to identify the gaps between where you are now and where you want to be and the strategies you need to fill those gaps. Gap analysis is useful at the beginning of your marketing planning process and when looking at your possible strategic options. It's essential when you're planning marketing tactics and action plans.

What is Gap Analysis?

GAP ANALYSIS IS...
... a technique that reveals the gaps between targets and actual performance and the strategies necessary to fill those gaps and help you to move from where you are now to where you want to be.

Why Do You Need Gap Analysis?

- To analyse the gaps between target and actual performance
- To fill those gaps with strategies
- To keep your marketing plan on track when you update it regularly

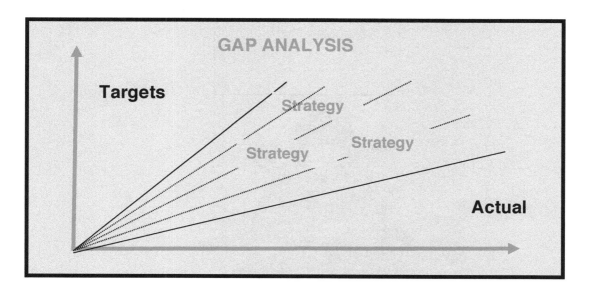

CHOOSE YOUR MARKETING STRATEGY

COMPETITIVE
MARKETING
STRATEGIES
How to Compete

Generic
Offensive
Defensive

MARKET GROWTH
STRATEGIES
(Ansoff Matrix)
Products & Markets

Market penetration
Market development
Product development
Diversification

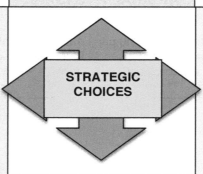

STRATEGIC
CHOICES

ORGANISATIONAL
STRATEGIES
How to Grow

Organic growth
Alliances
Joint ventures
Mergers and acquisitions
Networking
Culture change

DEATH STRATEGIES
How to Die

Do nothing
No growth

3. COMPETITIVE MARKETING STRATEGIES

There are 3 types of competitive strategies: generic, offensive and defensive. They are mutually exclusive and you can only choose one for each of your chosen market segments.

GENERIC STRATEGIES

Cost Leadership Strategy (Lower Pricing)

- Charge lower prices than your competitors
- Aim for higher sales volumes
- Include fewer product features
- Promote price advantage
- Make high profits depend on high volumes

Differentiation Strategy (Medium Pricing)

- Provide unique, innovative or superior products or services
- Differentiate from your competitors
- Add valued for the customer
- Don't be a follower, be a market leader

Niche Marketing Strategy (Higher Pricing)

- Target specific market segments or niches
- Customise products or services
- Add value for which the customers will pay
- Charge premium prices

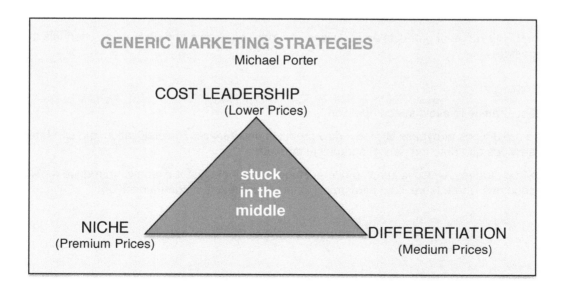

OFFENSIVE MARKETING STRATEGIES

Offensive marketing strategies can be used if you have direct competitors. These strategies should target customers who prefer the products and services of your competitors or those who are undecided. Identify your competitor's strengths and weaknesses, emphasise their weaknesses and play down their strengths. Monitor the effects of your offensive marketing campaigns by monitoring changes in your market share and researching customers' views, then abandon any strategies that aren't working.

Frontal Strategy

- Compete head on with your competitors
- Use a similar marketing mix as your competitors
- A very risky strategy

Flanking Strategy

- Challenge competitors where they are weak or non-existent
- Surprise competitors with your marketing campaigns
- Use social media marketing
- Innovate or re-invent the industry
- Enter new markets and new segments

Encirclement Strategy

- Multi-pronged strategy
- Dilute your competitor's ability to compete
- Expand your range of products and services into more segments and distribution channels than your competitors

Bypass Strategy

- Indirect strategy to avoid the competition
- There are 3 types of bypass strategy: new products and services, diversification into unrelated products and services and entering new geographical markets
- Leap-frog strategy, which is jumping over a stage in technology, for example, introduce mobile phones into countries where there is no infrastructure for other means of communication

Offensive Marketing Strategies
Kotler & Singh

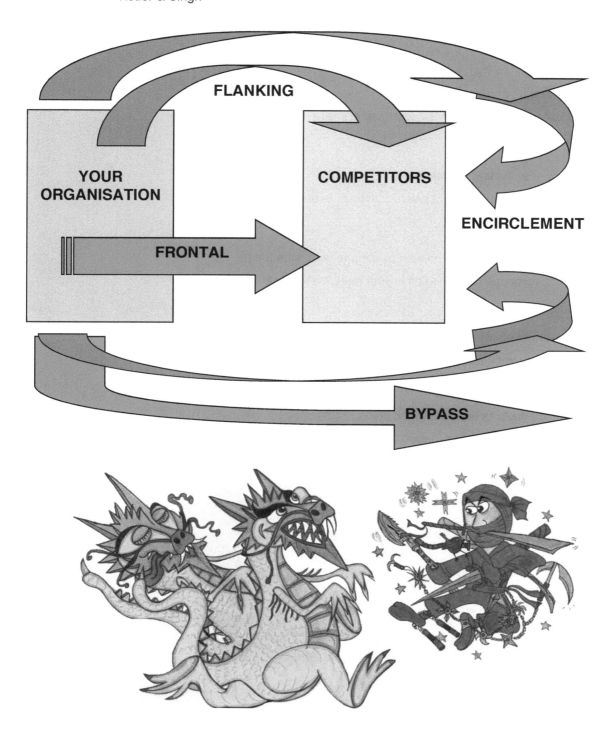

4. DEFENSIVE MARKETING STRATEGIES

Defensive marketing strategies are useful if your company has well established brands, products and services and a large market share. You only need to reinforce your marketing messages with your customers to ensure customer confidence. A well-built reputation, a strong brand and quality products and services make it difficult for a competitor to enter your markets.

Pre-Emptive Defence Strategy

- Strengthen your position with innovative new products and services
- Use flexibility as an advantage
- Don't hesitate, or you could lose your market share

Mobile Defence Strategy

- Enter new markets and segments
- Use product development and diversification to strengthen your position

Position Defence Strategy

- Concentrate your resources on your existing market segments
- Strengthen customer relationships in your market segments

Flank Defence Strategy

- Enter new markets with potential
- Secure your existing markets

Strategic Withdrawal Strategy

- Withdraw products or services which are not profitable
- Withdraw from markets and market segments that are not profitable

5. PRODUCT AND MARKET STRATEGIES (ANSOFF MATRIX)

The Ansoff Matrix

The Ansoff matrix was first published in the Harvard Business Review in 1957. Also known as product and marketing strategies, it provides a quick and simple way of planning your growth using a combination of existing and new markets and existing and new products and services. The Ansoff matrix shows 4 ways that your business can grow and will help you think about the risks associated with each option.

LOW COST
LOW RISK

	EXISTING PRODUCTS	**NEW PRODUCTS**
EXISTING MARKETS	**MARKET PENETRATION STRATEGY** **Maintain or increase existing market share** • Increase use by existing customers • Gain customers from competitors • Convert non-users to users By • Competitive pricing • Segmentation • The marketing mix	**PRODUCT DEVELOPMENT STRATEGY** **New products for existing markets** • Modify products adding new features • Develop different quality product lines • Offer new products and services By • Continuous research and development • Innovation
NEW MARKETS	**MARKET DEVELOPMENT STRATEGY** **New markets for current products or services** • Enter new market segments • Find new distribution channels By • Markets in new geographic areas • Different package sizes • Differential pricing policies for new segments	**DIVERSIFICATION STRATEGY** **New products for new markets** • Invest surplus resources By • Organic growth • Alliances and joint ventures • Mergers • Acquisitions • Takeovers

HIGH COST
HIGH RISK

YOUR ANSOFF MATRIX

	EXISTING PRODUCTS	**NEW PRODUCTS**
LOW COST LOW RISK		
EXISTING MARKETS	MARKET PENETRATION STRATEGY **Maintain or increase existing market share**	PRODUCT DEVELOPMENT STRATEGY **New products for existing markets**
NEW MARKETS	MARKET DEVELOPMENT STRATEGY **New markets for current products or services**	DIVERSIFICATION STRATEGY **New products for new markets**
		HIGH COST HIGH RISK

6. EVALUATE YOUR STRATEGIES

YOUR STRATEGY EVALUATION	Yes	No
• Do they contribute to your corporate objectives?		
• Are they ethical?		
• Are all your stakeholders and customers happy?		
• Does your organisation have the necessary competencies and resources to implement your strategies?		
• Do they exploit the strengths and opportunities identified in your SWOT analysis?		
• Do they eliminate challenges and reduce the threats identified in your SWOT analysis?		
• Are they consistent with your other strategies?		
• Do you have adequate control methods and contingency plans?		
• What are the risks? ·		
• How will your competitors respond?		
• What are your other options?		

Chapter 10 - MARKETING TACTICS

1. MARKETING TACTICS

Introduction

Now you've formulated your marketing objectives and planned your marketing strategy, it's time to implement your chosen strategies by converting them into action plans. Good marketing tactics focus your resources to ensure that your marketing strategies are implemented successfully.

MARKETING TACTICS ARE ...
... the methods and action plans used to implement your marketing strategies, and which will achieve your marketing objectives.

Why Plan Your Marketing Tactics?

- To implement your marketing strategies and achieve your marketing objectives
- To identify specific tasks and allocate responsibilities
- To plan the use of your resources
- To be more customer focused
- To make your products and services available at the right time, in the right place and at the right price
- To formulate a system of control and prepare contingency plans

2. THE MARKETING MIX (7Ps)

Introduction

The marketing mix, also known as the 7Ps, is a set of controllable variables that you use to influence your target markets. You need to design a specific and integrated marketing mix for each of your target market segments that satisfies their needs. Influences on the marketing mix include changes in the marketing environment, your markets and segments, the time of year, consumer or business-to-business markets and stages in the product lifecycle.

What is a Marketing Mix?

A MARKETING MIX IS...
… a combination of controllable elements of a marketing plan, which are specifically designed for each market segment's products and services. It's also called the 7Ps: product, price, place, promotion, people, process and physical evidence. The combination of the 7Ps satisfies customer needs in each segment.

Why Use a Marketing Mix?

- To maximise the use of your resources
- To communicate with each of your market segments
- To differentiate your business from your competitors
- To innovate and develop new products and services for each segment

3. MARKETING MIX TACTICS

PRODUCTS AND SERVICES

Your most important tactical tools are your products and services because they are the elements of the marketing mix that differentiate you from your competitors. You should continually innovate and develop new products and services using the latest research and development (R&D).

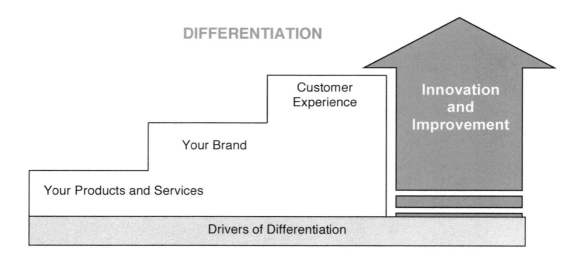

PRODUCT AND SERVICE TACTICS

- Define your business, the markets and customers in your chosen market segments
- Define your products and services
- Define your Unique Selling Propositions (USPs)
- Define the package of attributes, benefits and added value to the customer of each product and service

Market the Attributes and Customer Benefits

The attributes and benefits of your products and services position them as the best and help to differentiate them from your competitors' offerings. Attributes and benefits include quality, service, range of products and services, design and packaging, customer satisfaction and brand experience.

Define and describe your actual products, product lines and services, including their features and how they work. Then define and describe your augmented products and services, which include the attributes, benefits and added value, such as credit or warranties.

PRICE

Price is the only part of the marketing mix that involves revenue, not costs. Your objective is to maximise the gross margins generated by your products and services.

	Quality Low	Quality High
Low	ECONOMY	PENETRATION
High	SKIMMING	PREMIUM

PRICING TACTICS

Cost Based Pricing

- Cost + mark-up

Discount Pricing

- Encourages greater sales volume
- Benefits of early payment in exchange for discounts

Competitive Pricing

- Pricing your products and services lower than the competition

Promotional Pricing

- Promotional prices for a special promotion or for the introduction of new products and services
- Lowering prices to encourage new customers to try your products or services

New Product Pricing

- Penetration pricing involves lowering prices to gain market share and then raising the prices
- Skimming involves raising prices to recover investment and then lowering the prices

Place

DISTRIBUTION

Distribution is the delivery of products and services from the producer or provider to the customer. The most important factor is product and service availability.

Choose Your Methods and Channels of Distribution

- Weigh up the cost and benefit of each solution
- Calculate the number of intermediaries required, if any
- Consider direct distribution, including retail and ordering by mail, telephone and online

Factors to Consider

- Your customers and their locations
- Competitors' distribution strategies
- Nature of the product
- Stocking levels
- Ordering and invoicing systems
- Dealer relationships
- Depots and warehousing
- Channel benefits, costs and evaluation
- Choose storage or JIT (just in time production)

82

PROMOTION

Promotion is how an organisation communicates the attributes, values, features and benefits of its brands, products and services, in order to get attention from customers in its target markets and internal stakeholders, including employees.

It includes branding, advertising, PR, sales, e-marketing, promotions and exhibitions. The message needs to be attractive, consistent and integrated throughout the promotional mix. It must give customers a reason to prefer your offerings over those of your competitors.

TIP
Promotion is also known as marketing communications, or MARCOMS and should not be confused with marketing and marketing plans.

Your Promotional Objectives

- To create and increase the awareness and interest of your target audience
- To build and develop your brand image
- To position your brand, products and services as the first choice of customers in your target markets
- To generate enquiries and leads
- To remind customers of the attributes and benefits of your products and services
- To influence buyer behaviour

Promotional Tools

- Maximise the use of your marketing communication tools at a tactical level
- Use advertising, PR and personal selling
- Encourage customer referrals
- Write articles and publish them online and offline
- Build and manage a great website
- Use social media and blogging
- Network, attend events and conferences
- Give presentations and conduct teleclasses and webinars
- Host events, create promotions and have exhibition stands

ADVERTISING

What is Advertising?

ADVERTISING IS...
... the process of communicating to persuade an audience to purchase your products and services using paid media, including TV and radio adverts, print ads, billboards, product placement, the Internet, social media mobile devices. Ads are placed where they will reach the largest, most relevant audience.

Why Do You Need To Advertise?

- To reach wider audiences
- To reach your target audiences, target markets and potential customers
- To demonstrate the benefits, effectiveness and ease of use of your products and services
- To position yourself and build your brand image
- To change perceptions of your target audiences

ADVERTISING TACTICS

Promotion

- Develop an email database to send coupons or invite customers to special events
- Attach coupons to receipts that allow for savings on future purchases

Internet and Social Media Advertising

- Advertise on social media, including Linkedin, Facebook and Twitter
- Start and participate in blogs that a are relevant to your business
- Use the appropriate media to reach your target market and customers
- Integrate all media campaigns

Events and Exhibitions

- Increase sales by persuading potential customers to try your products or services
- Give incentives, including samples, discounts, deals, competitions, gifts and offers
- Use literature such as letters, brochures, leaflets and catalogues

PUBLIC RELATIONS – PR

What is Public Relations?

PUBLIC RELATIONS (PR) IS...
 ... a campaign or series of campaigns which present and maintain a positive image of your business and communicates key messages in the media to the public, including employees, customers, opinion leaders, suppliers, distributors and investors. It's an inexpensive and high-impact marketing tool, which relies on your time, energy and imagination.

What Does PR Include?

- Visual and printed communications
- Videos and television
- Personal communication, including meetings with journalists
- Media receptions and media packs
- Events, exhibitions and corporate hospitality

THE PR PROCESS

STEP 1   **Reach Your Target Audiences**
List the media that will reach your target audiences, including the internet, websites, social media, newspapers, advertising fliers, TV, radio and newsletters.

STEP 2   **Develop a Media Contact Database**
Determine where your news or announcement would best fit in each media. Develop a contact database with the names and details of appropriate editors, reporters, producers, websites and blog sites.

STEP 3   **Write Your PR Story**
Choose your PR topics. Decide what you want to communicate: an announcement, a change, a statement, an opinion or to reveal a finding. Choose a local angle or a national story. Make sure your information is newsworthy and not promotional. For maximum impact, choose 12 topics and one press release per month for a year. You can also report news when it happens or make announcements.

STEP 4   **Write and Send Your Press Releases**
Write one page press releases that include who, what, when, where, why and how. Also include background information, a quote from you or another person in your organisation and contact information. It doesn't have to be long or very detailed, if a reporter wants more of a story, they will contact you. Email your press release to everyone in your database, don't send it by snail mail! Due to the number of press releases generated, yours might not be published, but keep trying.

STEP 5   **Maximise the Impact of Your Press Releases**
Integrate your press releases with your other marketing communications tools. Post press releases on your website, use them for direct mail to customers and prospects, use them as handouts and in your leaflets. Be creative and you'll be surprised at the unique ways there are for you to generate interest in your business.

STEP 6   **Establish Media Relationships**
The more relationships you have with editors, reporters and producers in your targeted publications, the better your chances of getting publicity. The best time to do this is when you have a breaking news story that will make the biggest PR impact.

TIP
PR is not free advertising! it's not even free because someone has to pay for lunch.

PRESENTATIONS AND WEBINARS

- Design a powerpoint presentation
- Research local businesses and offer to give presentations
- Collect business cards
- Give teleclasses and webinars
- Use YouTube
- Build an e-list
- Don't forget to follow up

TELEMARKETING

What Is Telemarketing?

TELEMARKETING IS...
... the marketing of products and services using the telephone, teleconferencing or Skype.

Why Use Telemarketing?

- To increase the number of qualified leads
- To arrange appointments with key decision makers
- To promote your special offers
- To increase the amount and value of existing business by cross-selling and up-selling
- To grow your customer base and the level of new business
- To win new market segments
- To establish rapport with your customers and prospects
- To build relationships and customer loyalty
- To get immediate feedback
- For research

THE TELEMARKETING PROCESS

STEP 1   Set up Effective Systems

- Recruit and train your telemarketing team

- Build, manage and motivate your team

- Track, monitor and evaluate every aspect of your telemarketing campaigns

STEP 2   Your Database
- Build your database
- Continually update client and prospective client's information
- Give access to team members

STEP 3   Create the Right Culture
- Create a culture of learning, growth, creativity and innovation
- Include teamwork in your culture
- Involve everyone in your organisation in marketing and sales and offer them incentives, including commissions or recognition for achieving objectives

STEP 4   Create the Environment
- Work stations
- Noise control
- Computers and IT Systems
- Marketing Information System (MkIS)
- Write and test your telemarketing script

STEP 3   Go For It!!!

YOUR TELEMARKETING SCRIPT		
Open the Call	Identify the decision maker	
	Greeting	
	Identify your organisation	
	Identify yourself	
Get information	Verify phone number	
	Verify decision maker's name, title and spelling	
	Verifiy the address and spelling	
Voice and Telephone Manner	Positive attitude and polite manner	
	Maintain control of the call	
	Listen	
	Use effective communication skills	
	Maintain interest and be sympathetic	
	Use the right volume and pitch	
	Clarity, articulation and pronunciation	
	Tone – energy and enthusiasm	
	Pace the call	
Be Assertive	Get past the gatekeeper	
	Get through to the decision maker	
Listen and Respond	Provide accurate answers	
	Record important details	
	Use the customer's name	
	Respond to customer needs	
Upsell and Cross-sell	Use closed questions	
	Explore additional needs & opportunities	
	Focus on and present relevant benefits	
	Handle resistance & objections well	
Demonstrate Your Product Knowledge	Demonstrate extensive product knowledge	
	Demonstrate familiarity with prices, features and benefits	
	Demonstrate credibility and self-confidence	
	Answer any questions	
Make an Appointment	Gain commitment	
	Make the appointment	
	Confirm the appointment, time, date and location	
Close the Call	Thank the prospect or customer by name	
	Maintain a courteous manner	

PERSONAL SELLING

What Is Personal Selling?

PERSONAL SELLING IS...
 ... the process of selling a product or service, usually by face-to-face communication, personal correspondence or a personal telephone, Skype or teleconferencing conversation.

TIPS
• A personal sales message should be specifically targeted to individual prospective clients • Alter your message if the desired behaviour does not occur • Personal selling should be supported by marketing communications to strengthen its impact

Factors to Consider

- Size and structure of your salesforce, whether made up of employees or agents
- Remuneration, the salary and commission mix
- Training and motivation
- Support from the whole organisation
- Evaluation and control

Selling to the Business-to-Business Market

- Personal selling is very important in the business-to-business market
- The process of decision making is more complicated
- There are different needs and technical issues
- The value of purchases is higher

Tasks for Your Salesforce

- Establishing customer needs
- Helping customers to satisfy their needs with your products and services
- Collecting information and marketing intelligence
- Prospecting for new markets and new customers and following sales leads
- Communicating information to existing and potential customers
- Delivering sales presentations
- Selling your organisation's goods and services
- Personal services, including consultancy, technical, finance and delivery
- Customer care and building and maintaining customer relationships
- Networking and selling within your supply chain
- Getting referrals from customers

Impress Your Prospects

- Give them samples and any information to your customers that they may value
- Make the sale come alive with visual presentations or anything that will add excitement
- Try mystery shopping to experience how it feels to be your customer
- Don't use pressure tactics – let them feel free to make decisions in their own time

The Service Marketing Mix

Every business, whether it only offers products or services, should also be providing a service to its customers. In addition to the marketing mix of a product the service marketing mix includes product, price, place and promotion. The service element is intangible, so the marketing mix needs to be extended to include people, process and physical evidence.

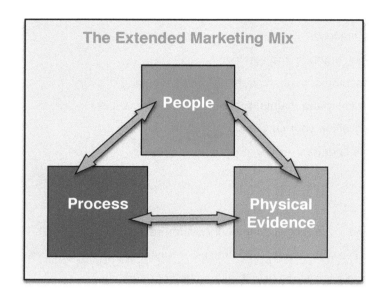

PEOPLE

People are essential to providing a service. It's important to recruit the right people and provide appropriate training to create a competitive advantage. Your customers will make judgments about the quality, provision and delivery of the service based on their interactions with the people who represent your organisation including directors, employees and organisational culture.

PROCESS

The process is the system used to deliver an efficient and consistent service that will create customer loyalty and confidence in your company. This includes customer service, response to complaints and customer satisfaction.

PHYSICAL EVIDENCE

Physical evidence is where the service is delivered and will distinguish you from your competitors. It can be used to charge a premium price for your service and establish a positive customer experience. Customers will make judgements about your organisation based on the physical evidence, including recommendations, premises, buzz, gifts and vouchers.

MARKETING MIX PLAN (EXAMPLE)

Product	Price	Place	Promotion	People	Process	Physical Evidence
Design	Penetration	Retail	Advertising	Directors	Service	Stories
Technology	Cost plus	Wholesale	Recommendation	Employees	Complaints	Premises
Usability	Lost leader	E-tail	Special offers	Culture	Response	Buzz
Usefulness		Local	Gifts	Consumers		Gifts
Value		Export	Website	Customers		Vouchers
Quality		Internet	Social media	Clients		
Brand						
Warranty						

YOUR MARKETING MIX PLAN

Product	Price	Place	Promotion	People	Process	Physical Evidence
Design						
Technology						
Usability						
Usefulness						
Value						
Quality						
Brand						
Warranty						

Chapter 11 - DIGITAL MARKETING

1. DIGITAL MARKETING

Introduction

The Internet has changed our lives, it makes it possible to access and share information, photos and videos and communicate with people and organisations all over the world. It has contributed to the decline of traditional media. Marketing using the Internet is called digital marketing or eMarketing.

Digital marketing campaigns need to be planned, the same as any other marketing plan, using Ninja marketing tools. The difference is the media and a successful strategy depends on making the most effective use of digital media.

The main objective of digital marketing is to direct users to your website so that you can convert them into customers. The development of your website and social media sites is the center of all your online marketing activities. You need to drive traffic to your sites and build relationships with your target audience by creating a fantastic website, videos, banner adverts and great social media sites. You can then track and analyse to monitor results and improve your campaigns.

What is Digital Marketing?

DIGITAL MARKETING IS ...

... the same as marketing but uses the power of the Internet, which provides a new environment for customers and potential customers to connect with businesses, brands and each other.

Why Use Digital Marketing?

- Because it gives your brands the opportunity to build tailored, optimised brand experiences

- Because it's measurable and the best way of tracking the effectiveness of marketing campaigns, results and trends

- Because it adapts the principles of traditional marketing, using the opportunities and challenges offered by technology and digital media

- Because it allows you to communicate and interact with existing and potential customers worldwide 24/7

2. YOUR WEBSITE

Introduction

The success of your websites depends on strong planning and focusing on the needs of your target audience. Your websites should be accessible and usable, search engine optimised, shareable and look professional. Key considerations include, well thought out information, clear navigation and functionality that works across all browsers. The design should enhance the user experience and guide visitors through your website, not distract them from their goals.

What is a Website?

A WEBSITE IS...
... a set of web pages that contains text and images and has been formatted with HTML instructions and is hosted on a server with a domain name and is accessible on the Internet.

Why Do You Need a Website?

- Because most people who are looking for a product or service start by looking online
- To have an online presence which is visible on computers and mobile devices, including mobile phones and tablets
- Because customers make purchasing decisions based on online information
- Because online business involves lower transaction costs
- To use the most cost effective way of marketing and attracting new clients
- To enable you to reach a wider, international audience
- To enable your customers to buy your products and services online
- To improve customer services and the customer experience
- To be open for business 24/7
- To have higher visibility on all the search engines using the right keywords
- To allow your customers to access information about your products and services
- To have the equivalent of a catalogue delivered to every computer in the world
- To link your website with social media in order to build your audience

Critical Success Factors – CFSs for Your Website

Ease of Access
Ensure that your website is compatible across all browsers and all mobile devices to increase accessibility and overcome barriers which prevent access.

User Friendliness
Use links, search buttons, menus and sitemaps to make your website more user friendly and easier to navigate.

Search Engine Optimisation (SEO)
Make your website easier to find by searching by using methods which indicate your location on the Internet, provide information about a web page and which are not seen by users. Use keywords and key phrases which describe your website and its pages to search engines and are what users enter into search engines to find websites.

The Right Links
Link your website to social media and other relevant and credible sites to make it more discoverable.

Credibility
Make your website look professional. Display your contact details, feature testimonials, logos of associations and awards and link to credible third parties. An "About Us" page helps viewers to understand your business.

Design for Sharing
Build your website for sharing and link it to social media sites such as Facebook, Linkedin and Twitter and display their icons on your website.

Visual Design and Online Copy
Ensure that the visual design of your website is beautiful, professional, useful and compelling to viewers by appealing to their interests and needs. Use your logo. Provide interesting content, update regularly and ensuring that your site does not contain errors. Optimise your copy for search engines by researching and using keywords and key phrases.

Keywords and Key Phrases
Use keywords and key phrases that are relevant to your website and used by your potential customers. Words and phrases that describe your website and are accessed by text reading browsers and are what users enter into a search engine to find websites. Your objective is to have your website rank high in the search engines for its target keywords. In Pay Per Click (PPC) advertising, the right keywords achieve better results.

A Content Management System
Content Management System (CMS) is the system used to manage and update the content of your website. Your site should have an inbuilt search engine friendly CMS which supports the goals and functions of your website, your brand and your business and allows you to edit and add content to your site easily.

Testing and Launching
Now it's time to test your new website and then take it live! Testing is an important part of website development and design. Your website needs to be tested in all browsers and mobile devices to make sure that it looks and works properly. All links should be tested and it's always a good idea to have a final check of all the copy before it goes live. Now you need drive traffic to your newly launched site.

3. MOBILE WEBSITES AND MOBILE APPS (APPLICATIONS)

Mobile phones, tablets and other mobile devices are changing the way we access the Internet and communicate. Mobile technology is continually developing and new and better features are put into smaller and smaller devices. They enable us to create and access information from almost anywhere in the world. You can reach more of your target audience through their mobile phone and as mobile devices get more powerful you can create richer mobile experiences.

There are two methods for developing content for mobile phones: mobile websites and mobile applications, better known as apps. Mobile websites enable users to access information from anywhere in the world if their mobile phone has a browser and an Internet connection. Mobile websites need to be designed for mobile phones. Apps are designed separately for each mobile device and platform. The best choice for your business depends on your main objectives and you your may need both.

What's the Difference Between a Mobile Website and an App?

	MOBILE WEBSITES	MOBILE APPS
Description	Websites that are designed for smaller hand held devices and touch screens	Applications that are downloaded and installed on a mobile device without using a browser
Mobile devices and platforms	Any mobile device with Internet access and a browser	Mobile device and platform specific
Access	Found through searches and links and can only be accessed using an Internet enabled mobile device and can be shared	Only found through stores and once downloaded can be accessed without connection to the Internet
Use	Market driven and used to deliver a range of information and establish a broad mobile presence	Designed for mobile devices and interactive, to help users perform specific tasks or functions, such as looking at recipes, playing mobile games, banking and ticket purchasing
Target audience	Great for targeting broad groups of users and for achieving specific marketing objectives	Ideal for reaching a niche or targeted audience and to pull customers to your mobile sites
Design and build	Built once and adapted for each mobile device or platform	Designed for particular mobile devices and rebuilt for each mobile platform, adapted to software updates and operates more like a computer program than a website

Advantages of a Mobile Website

Instant Availability
It's available using a browser on any mobile device that is connected to the Internet. An app needs to be downloaded and installed before they can be viewed or used.

Compatibility
Once developed, it can be viewed and used on any mobile device. An app requires a different version to be developed for each type of platform and device.

Instantly Upgradable and Updatable
It's more dynamic and flexible for updating content and changes are immediately visible. Updating an app requires the user to download the update on each type of mobile device.

Easily Findable
It's much easier to find than an app because pages are displayed in search results and listed in directories. An app is only visible through app stores.

Designed for Sharing
It's easily shared using a link by email, text message or social media. An app can't be shared.

Broader Reach
It has a greater reach because it's more easily accessible than an app and can be easily shared.

Longer Shelf Life
It has a longer life than an app, which only has a short life on a user's mobile device.

More Time and Cost Effective
It's more time and cost effective to design and develop than an app.

Easier to Support and Sustain
It's easier to support and sustain than an app, which involves development, upgrades, testing and compatibility for each mobile device and platform.

Advantages of a Mobile App

Interactivity
It's more interactive than a mobile website for tasks and functions, such as playing games on mobile devices.

Can be Personalised
Users can personalise it for regular use.

Effective for Calculating or Reporting
It can use data and make complex calculations, charts and reports, such as banking or investment.

Offline Access
Contents and performing functions can be accessed without a network or Internet connection.

4. SOCIAL MEDIA

Introduction

Social media is about collaboration and sharing ideas, information, photos and videos. It's increasingly responsible for a lot of the content available on the Internet because it allows anyone with an Internet connection to create and share content easily and without cost. It's dynamic because it has many participants, who can interact with each other to either enhance or detract from your brand image.

Social media is designed for sharing to make it easy to send and make comments, either free or with no high costs involved. Comments, sharing and viewing can be tracked and measured. Comparing social media to traditional media is probably the best way to understand it.

What is Media?

MEDIA IS ...
... the plural of medium and is the main channels of mass communication for news, education, data or promotional messages and includes broadcasting, print, social media and the Internet.

Your Message and Media

- Must allign a consistent message with your brand and integrate it with all your promotions
- Your choice of media must be right for your target audiences
- Should be cost effective
- Needs to emphasise the attributes and benefits of your brand, products and services
- Should be innovative, creative and better than your competition

What is Social Media?

SOCIAL MEDIA IS ...
... the same as media but a different means of communication by which people and communities interact, create, share, discuss and exchange information and ideas through Internet based networks.

Why Use Social Media?

- Because Internet users spend increasingly more time on social media sites than any other type of site
- To build your online brand image and personality and allow your audience to become involved
- To integrate your website and email marketing activities with social media spaces
- Because it's more compatible with mobile devices and mobile transactions are increasing
- To create and engage online communities
- To promote your reputation, advertise, build awareness
- To communicate directly with customers and support and strengthen customer relationships
- To generate leads, sales and increase your market share
- To track and analyse customer feedback

YOUR MEDIA STRATEGY			
Media	Use	Target Audiences	Message
Advertising			
Public Relations (PR)			
LinkedIn			
Facebook			
Twitter			
Website			
Mobile Website			

5. BLOGGING

What is Blogging?

BLOGGING IS ...
... a method of broadcasting your views and comments on an online personal journal, your website or a dedicated blogging site, with links that you can provide.

Why Blog?

- It's is an important contemporary part of marketing communications which helps profile your brand
- To have a higher visibility on search engines because they perceive your content to be fresh and relevant
- To optimise contact with your target audiences and engage with them on a consistent basis
- To feed search engines with content that is optimised around certain topics (as signalled by using relevant keywords and key phrases)
- To give people and organisations opportunitites to link to your sites and improve your search engiine optimsation of your site
- To position yourself in your sector by providing information and interest for your customers and prospects
- To express your point of view and share opinions on topics that you think are important
- To increase lead generation and customer acquisition
- To provide people who follow you in social spaces like Linkedin, Facebook and Twitter a way to better understand your business and your brand
- To get referrals from clients and affiliates
- To offer your clients and fans an opportunity to give you feedback and comments

Chapter 12 - ACTION PLANS

1. THE MARKETING BUDGET

Introduction

Your marketing budget and timelines are the most important factors in setting up your marketing campaign. Your budget should contain an estimate of the cost of each marketing activity over a defined time period.

This will enable you to monitor the cost of each marketing activity and to compare the actual cost against your budget. You can then make the appropriate changes if necessary.

What is a Marketing Budget?

A MARKETING BUDGET IS…
… an estimate of the cost of your marketing activities phased over a defined time period, such as your company's financial year.

TIP – DON'T BE INFLEXIBLE
Your marketing budget shouldn't be fixed or inflexible, you may need to throw in another unplanned campaign or event!

Why Do You Need a Marketing Budget?

- To understand, monitor and control the costs of your marketing activities
- To stop you overspending
- To see whether your budget is helping you achieve your marketing objectives
- To know if you need to modify your marketing plan
- To project and get a better return on your marketing investment (ROI)
- To co-ordinate your marketing activities, track results and keep them on target

THE MARKETING BUDGET PROCESS

STEP 1   **Plan the Effective Use of Your Marketing Resources**

Your annual budget for marketing costs must include your allocation of fixed costs and an appropriate allowance for all the planned marketing activities necessary to implement your marketing strategies. You will also need to provide a contingency factor in your activity budget to meet the cost of any unexpected events.

STEP 2   **Define Your Marketing Activities**

Have a strategy for targeting your market segments and customers. Define your planned marketing activities over the period of your marketing campaigns and plan the phases and the resources required for each phase of the activity. The key is to decide how to effectively reach your target markets and what media is appropriate.

STEP 3   **Define the Costs of Your Marketing Activities**

Formulate detailed budgets, plans and procedures for each marketing activity. Prepare a schedule detailing all the costs of each marketing activity, phased over the relevant period of time. This will include the fixed costs for your staff, your allocation of the overheads used in operating the marketing function and all the variable costs, including market research, contractors, marketing communications, agency fees and media costs.

STEP 3   **Evaluate and Control Your Marketing Budget**

It's important to monitor the performance of your marketing activities. Plan how to track expenditures, the costs of acquiring customers and compare your performance before and after each phase of your marketing activity. Monitor your actual marketing expenditure against your budget regularly to determine whether you are getting the predicted return from each of your marketing activities. If some part of your marketing plan isn't working, make the necessary changes.

MARKETING BUDGET PLANNING

Your marketing budget should summarise your expenditure on your marketing strategies for each quarter, itemising your expenditure by month and by marketing strategy. Enter the total in the last column for each quarter.

Calculate Your Marketing Expenditures as a Percentage of Sales Revenue

Express your marketing expenditures as a percentage of total sales or revenue, divide the marketing expenditure of each month by the total sales for that month.

EXAMPLE OF A MARKETING BUDGET				
Marketing Budget	January	February	March	Quarterly Expenditure
Allocated overheads				
Payroll and training				
Website				
Online campaigns				
Direct marketing				
Advertising				
Trade shows, exhibitions and conferences				
Catalogs and brochures				
Other				
Other				
Other				
Other				
CALCULATION OF MARKETING BUDGET AS % OF SALES				
Marketing budget spent				
Total Sales				
Marketing as a % of sales				

104

Track The Cost Of Generating Leads and Customer Acquisition

Most of your marketing strategies will bring in some leads and some will generate more than others. You need to track the leads back to the source to determine the cost of customer acquisition to discover which strategy is most cost effective.

Use the following table to outline the cost of customer acquisitions based on sample marketing strategies from your budget. Analyse each campaign to see how many leads were generated for each month of the quarter and divide the total marketing expenditure by the number of leads generated to see the cost per lead generated.

Marketing strategy For Each Quarter	Online campaigns	Offline campaigns	Advertising	Trade shows exhibitions & conferences
Month 1				
Month 2				
Month 3				
Leads generated in Quarter				
Average cost of lead				

YOUR CRITICAL SUCCESS FACTORS (CFSs)

- Increasing your return on your marketing expenditure
- Reducing the cost of customer acquisition
- Increasing the number of leads generated by each marketing activity
- Tracking the source of your leads
- Determining your average cost per lead
- Focusing on the most cost effective approach to finding new customers

2. YOUR MARKETING TIMELINES

Introduction

Finish off your marketing tactics by plotting your timelines on a Gantt chart. Your marketing timelines help you to monitor the results of your tactics, compare results during times when you've implemented certain marketing activities and check for growth to see if there was an impact.

What is a Marketing Timeline?

A MARKETING TIMELINE IS...
… a method of showing marketing events in chronological order. It's typically a Gantt Chart, which is a bar graph with labelled bars and dates and events shown on dates when they are meant to occur. 

Why Do You Need Marketing Timelines?

- To map the activities that will achieve your marketing and sales objectives
- To monitor your budget and timelines
- To know if your marketing tactics are effective in driving sales
- To plan ahead and maintain a steady pace
- To track and compare sales activity on a regular basis
- To see if there is growth in your target markets
- To understand the impact of your marketing strategies
- To give you time to implement contingency plans, if required

Components of Your Timeline

- Market and competitor research
- Quantitative analysis
- Strategic planning
- Internal and external communications planning
- Positioning and branding
- Promotion, sales and sales support
- Analysis and reviews of your campaigns
- Extra time for the unexpected

Your Critical Success Factors (CFSs)

- Planning, planning, planning
- Allowing enough time to get it right first time and team buy-in
- KISS – Keep It Short and Simple, start with a basic plan
- Allowing enough time for production
- Creating a detailed rollout plan
- Tracking and measuring results regularly
- Getting everyone in your organisation involved

THE MARKETING TIMELINE PROCESS

STEP 1   Plan Your Marketing Strategies
Planning is the most important step in the process and should always be done first.

STEP 2   Your Marketing Message
This is the main success factor and the key to reaching you target market segments. Your marketing message needs be right before you take any action.

STEP 3   Your Timeline and Costs
Work backwards from your launch date, identifying the timing and costs of each element of your marketing activity.

STEP 4   Your Key Tasks
Identify key tasks, allocate them to team members and communicate them to the whole team.

STEP 5   Define Deadlines
Use all the marketing tools that you need and define the production deadlines. Set realistic time frames and draft a time plan with approximate times. Update it when the dates are confirmed or the timeline changes, distribute it to everyone in the team and get feedback.

STEP 6   External Marketing Activities
Create a plan for your marketing activities and set the dates for each stage.

STEP 7   Internal Marketing Activities
Get buy-in from all members of your project and sales teams. Keep them in the loop and inform them of your rollout plans and their tasks and responsibilities. Encourage feedback.

STEP 8   Marketing Tools
Use every tool in your marketing toolkit to achieve your objectives and ensure results.

STEP 9   Tactical Rollout
Work with team members to plan a successful rollout strategy.

STEP 10   Measure Results
Establish benchmarks and record monthly and quarterly sales to compare with your costs. Track results and hold team members accountable for their performance. Prepare contingency plans.

3. GANTT CHART

Introduction

Gantt charts are commonly used to manage projects or activities and to implement a marketing strategy. A Gantt chart is a graphic representation that will show you the amount of time tasks should take, the costs, how they interact and who is responsible for each task.

These charts enable you to see the order in which tasks should be carried out, identify overlaps and monitor their progress against estimated time frames. This helps in the planning phase and keeps your action plan and marketing plan on track.

What is a Gantt Chart?

A GANTT CHART IS...
... a horizontal bar chart, developed by Henry Gantt, which illustrates a project's schedule, including the start and finish dates of each phase, the associated costs and a definition of the tasks, responsibilities and their relationships.

Why Do You Need a Gantt Chart?

- To schedule, monitor and communicate plans, status and tasks within your marketing activities
- To plot the steps, sequence, duration and process of each activity
- To show which tasks depend on the completion of previous tasks

GANTT CHART

THE GANTT CHART PROCESS

STEP 1   **Key Tasks**
Identify and define the key tasks required to successfully complete the project.

STEP 2   **Key Milestones**
Identify the key milestones, make a list or drawing of a flowchart, storyboard or diagram.

STEP 3   **Timing and Costs**
Identify the time and costs needed for each task. Be realistic.

STEP 4   **Sequence**
Identify the tasks that need to be finished before the next ones can start, which tasks can happen at the same time, any overlaps and those that need to be completed for each milestone.

STEP 5   **Horizontal Time Axis**
Draw a horizontal time axis along the top or bottom, with an appropriate scale for the time frames and costs (days or weeks).

STEP 6   **Vertical Axis**
Draw a vertical axis down the left side and write each task and milestone in order.

STEP 7   **Plot Activities and Events**
Draw a bar on the timeline for a period of tasks or activities, align the left of the bar with the time the activity starts and align the right end with the time the activity ends. For specific events, draw a diamond under the time of the event.

STEP 8   **Ensure that Every Task of the Project is on Your Chart**

How to Use Your Gantt Chart

- As events and activities are completed, mark the boxes and bars
- For tasks in progress, estimate how far along you are and mark on the bar
- Place a vertical marker to show where you are on the timeline and costs
- You can create additional columns showing details, such as the amount of time the task is expected to take, resources or skill levels needed or the people responsible
- Plot regular reviews
- Keep your Gantt chart up to date as the project proceeds to manage and avoid problems
- You can indicate critical points on the chart by outlining the bars with bold or coloured outlines
- Computer software can simplify the construction and any updating of a Gantt chart

PROJECT MANAGEMENT SOFTWARE

You can manage larger or more complex projects using one of the widely available project management software products. These will enable you to:

- Construct detailed timelines and budgets
- Phase your resource requirements
- Identify critical actions on which progress depends
- Prioritise tasks
- Allocate resources and responsibilities
- Generate clear and concise reports

EXAMPLE OF A GANTT CHART

EXAMPLE OF A GANTT CHART												
Project	**Months**											
	1	2	3	4	5	6	7	8	9	10	11	12
Presentation	█											
Review Data		█	█									
Draft Key Elements			█	█								
Audit				█	█	█						
Research												
Marketing Planning						█	█					
Report and Presentation								█				
Implement Plan									█	█	█	█

YOUR GANTT CHART

Gantt charts make it easy to track and chart project timelines and budgets. There are many ways to create a Gantt chart, including using our template or create your own, using a spreadsheet or buying project management software.

YOUR GANTT CHART

Project	Months											
	1	2	3	4	5	6	7	8	9	10	11	12

NOTES

Chapter 13 - MANAGE

1. EVALUATION

Introduction

Even if your marketing plan is carefully formulated, there is no guarantee that it will produce the maximum return on your marketing investment. The marketing environment is constantly changing and your marketing plan will need to be evaluated and adapted over time in order for it to remain effective.

You should evaluate marketing performance in relation to your marketing plan, including sales analysis, market share analysis, marketing expenses to sales ratios, attitude tracking, profitability and efficiency.

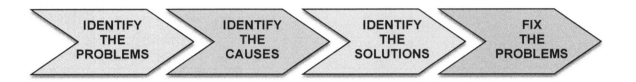

What is Marketing Evaluation?

MARKETING EVALUATION IS …
… the process of analysing the performance of completed or ongoing marketing activities to assess their effectiveness and efficiency

Why Do You Need to Evaluate Your Marketing Performance?

- To keep your marketing plan and budget on track
- To assess the effectiveness of your promotional activities
- To ensure that you are using the most effective media
- To maximise the return on your marketing investment
- To review what you've achieved (or not achieved)
- To compare actual performance against your plans and standards
- To use the information in the next planning cycle
- To change or eliminate unproductive marketing tactics

Criteria for Evaluating Your Marketing Performance

- Revenue from products and services by segment
- Impact of marketing activities
- Improvements in market share
- Cost of marketing activities as a percentage of sales revenue
- Feedback from customer surveys
- Marketing expenditure against budgets
- Performance against targets

2. CONTROL

Introduction

Marketing control is comparing actual performance against your marketing objectives and standards. Any significant deviation requires investigation and appropriate action. Set parameters for diversions and only take action if they are exceeded.

What Is Control?

CONTROL IS ...
... the process of setting standards, monitoring and measuring performance and taking appropriate, corrective action if necessary.

Why Do You Need Control?

- To ensure that your marketing plan is working
- To monitor and report performance
- To compare performance against your objectives
- To meet your performance standards
- To identify any unsatisfactory performance
- To take appropriate action to correct significant deviations

Some Methods of Monitoring and Measuring

- Market share analysis
- Sales analysis
- Quality controls
- Budgets, cash flow
- Ratio analysis
- Market research
- Your Marketing Information Systems (MkIS)
- Feedback from customers, satisfaction surveys and customer loyalty programmes
- Your Customer Relationship Management (CRM) systems
- Performance of your marketing mix

CONTROL TECHNIQUES

Financial Performance Analysis

- Compare budgets to actual financials, including assets, revenue, gross margin, expenses, operating costs and cash flow
- Use ratios to understand and take control of your marketing plan and monitor your performance
- Carry out a cost-volume-profit analysis

Strategic Performance Analysis

- Monitor the size and growth of your market segments with a market and sales analysis
- Analyse your market share compared to your competitors
- Monitor your quality controls
- Use market research, marketing audits, meetings and discussions to gather information

Tactical Effectiveness Analysis

- Monitor progress in all areas of the marketing mix
- Monitor and compare agreed targets and objectives with actual performance

CORRECTIVE ACTION

- Take action to improve performance if it doesn't meet standards and targets
- Review and change performance standards, targets and objectives where necessary
- Use a combination of both
- When performance meets or exceeds targets carry on with the plan
- Exploit opportunities in the market

3. CONTINGENCY PLANNING

Introduction

Contingency plans make it possible for you to react quickly to changes in the environment. It enables you to minimise threats or damage to your business and exploit good market conditions. Contingency planning requires creative and strategic thinking and you to anticipate what events could affect your business. You can create 'what if' scenarios, which describe possible threats that are likely to occur and create plans to address them.

What is a Contingency Plan?

A CONTINGENCY PLAN IS ...
... a plan to address any unexpected events, to help manage risk and avoid negative consequences to your business.

Why Do You Need Contingency Plans?

- To maintain your business operations in a crisis – this is your main goal
- To prepare for disruptive events, including the loss of data, people, customers, and suppliers
- To gain an insight into the risks that could affect your business
- To enable you to respond quickly and effectively to unexpected events

Maintain Your Plan

- Review and update the plan on a regular basis
- Carry out more thorough reviews if there are any significant changes
- Reassess the risks to your business
- Communicate the plan to everyone in your organisation
- Ensure the plan is maintained and kept up to date and any changes communicated to staff
- Allocate roles and responsibilities
- Provide training, conduct drills and assess the results
- Make changes where necessary
- Test any changes if the plan is modified and distribute revised plans

THE CONTINGENCY PLANNING PROCESS

STEP 1   Ensure That You're Insured

You can insure against most business risks and liabilities, including the loss of profits and any increased cost as the result of a disaster. Some insurance is mandatory, such as public and employer's liability Take professional advice about additional types of insurance that are necessary for your business.

STEP 2   Risk Assessment

Identify all the potential risks to your critical functions and operations. Prioritise and rate each in terms of their impact and probability. Plan mitigation strategies and formulate contingency plans for the risks that have the highest probability and impact rating first and the lowest risk last.

STEP 3   Response Strategy and Action Plans

Plan your response strategy and action plans, including contact details of emergency services and other specialists. The first milestone is the immediately after an incident.

STEP 4   Identify the Trigger

Decide what will cause you to implement the plan and what actions you need to take and when. Allocate responsibilities for each stage of the process.

STEP 5   Prepare a Plan B

Determine if you can operate with restricted resources or reduced capabilities.

STEP 6   Involve Your Staff

Involve all your staff. Get feedback to ensure that roles and responsibilities are understood in order to deal with any potential issues.

STEP 7   Define Success

Define what you will need to do to return to business as usual.

STEP 8   Include Contingency Plans

Make contingency planning part of your business's operations and include standard operation procedures. Communicate the plans to everyone in your organisation, provide training for these plans and keep everyone up to date on changes.

STEP 9   Reduce and Manage Risks

Look for opportunities to reduce and manage risks, wherever possible.

STEP 10   Identify Operational Inefficiencies

Identify operational inefficiencies and plan performance improvement.

STEP 11   Test the Plan

Regularly test the plan with everyone involved. Get feedback, record the results, then audit your plan and identify areas that need improvement.

117

Chapter 14 – GO FOR IT !!!

1. YOUR MARKETING PLAN TEMPLATE

Introduction

This Marketing Plan can be used as a strategic planning tool for a planned or existing business, or to present as part of a business plan for investment capital or business loan. You can use all of it or use any sections that are appropriate to your business or the purpose.

2. CONTENTS

1. Executive Summary

1.1 Brief Description of the Business

- Name, address, telephone, email and website
- Directors
- Shareholders
- Business activities

1.2 Mission Statement

- Define the purpose of the business
- Express what the company is aiming to achieve
- Focus on long-term direction
- Include products, services, markets, customer needs and technology
- Simple, honest and easy to grasp in order to motivate staff and customers

1.3 Marketing Team, Key Staff and Job Responsibilities

- The marketing team should be experienced and have demonstrated success
- Brief resume of each senior member of the marketing team and their function and areas of responsibility within the company
- Include an organisational chart
- Brief description of the marketing team as it is now and as it will be in the future
- A small company may consider outsourcing to a marketing consultancy

2. Situation Analysis

2.1 Your Market Segments

- Demographics
- Needs and trends
- Size and growth
- Key success factors

2.2 External Environment (Macro)

- **P**olitical
- **E**conomic
- **S**ocial
- **T**echnological

2.3 Competitor Analysis

- List main competitors
- Market share of each
- Competitors' products and services
- What are their strategies, strengths and weaknesses?
- How has the company compared to the competition?
- What is the outlook for any changes?
- What are the company's competitive advantages, the resources and strengths compared to the competitors?
- What does the company do better than the competition?
- What is the company's sustainable competitive advantage?
- What barriers to entry are there?
- Is the market dominated by 2 or 3 major competitors, a few major competitors, hundreds of smaller companies and lots of regional brands, or is the market very fragmented with no one company dominating?

2.4 Customer Analysis

- Demographics and buyer behaviour
- Opportunities for existing and potential customers

2.5 Performance – Past and Present

- Market share and market growth
- Net profit margin and ratio analysis
- Current situation of each of the 7Ps

3. Marketing Objectives

3.1 Performance Goals

- Short, medium and long-term
- By market segments
- By products and services

3.2 Strengths, Weaknesses, Opportunities and Threats – SWOT Analysis

- Describe internal strengths and capabilities
- Describe internal weaknesses and resource deficiencies
- Describe external opportunities and threats
- Explain how the company can use strengths to overcome weaknesses
- Explain how the company can convert threats to opportunities

4. Segmentation, Targeting and Positioning

4.1 Targeting Primary, Secondary and Tertiary Segments

- Segment the market
- Size and attractiveness of each segment
- Target your chosen market segments
- Expected segment growth and revenue
- Segment share

4.2 Positioning Strategies for Each Segment

- Value positioning
- Quality positioning
- Demographic positioning
- Competitive positioning
- Rationale for each

5. Branding

5.1 Brand Image and Personality

- Brand name
- Logo - the marque or symbol of the brand
- Strapline - a memorable phrase that summarises the attributes of the products, services, brand and market position

5.2 The Brand Experience

- Define the brand experience
- Promote the benefits, not the features

5.3 Customer Loyalty Programmes

- Describe customer loyalty programme
- Include benefits and rewards for customer loyalty

5.4 Marketing Objectives

- What you want to achieve
- SMART objectives: sustainable, measurable, achievable, realistic and timeframes

6. Marketing Strategies

The marketing strategies are how to achieve marketing objectives and should include every element in the marketing mix, or 7Ps: product, price, place or distribution, promotion, people, process and physical evidence.

6.1 Choose Your Strategies

- Generic strategies (choose one) – cost leadership, differentiation, or niche marketing
- Growth strategies (Ansoff)
- Marketing mix strategies (7Ps)
- Rationale for each

6.2 The Marketing Mix - 7Ps

- Product, price, place, promotion, people, process, physical evidence
- Description for each
- Proposed strategy, tactics and action plans for each

6.3 International Markets

- The international market segments that you intend to target
- Modifications to your marketing mix (7Ps)

6.4 Marketing Plans

- How will the company convince customers to choose their products and services over competitors? On price, perceived value, status, service level, economy, convenience?
- How much is this all going to cost?

6.5 Market Segmentation and Target Markets

- What are the needs and expectations of customers in the target markets?
- Select the market segments that are potentially the most profitable
- Select the needs and expectations that the company has a strong ability to satisfy
- What value could the company provide to its customers?
- What customer needs could be satisfied?
- How can the company productively and profitably serve these needs?

6.6 Product and Services Strategy

- Describe the company's products and services, including attributes and benefits
- Can include drawings or photos
- Describe and explain any changes or improvements in the products or services which have occurred or are projected to change significantly
- If a product or service is still in the research and development stage, describe how far it's come and what steps remain to get it ready for market
- Compare the company's products and services with those offered by the competition
- Include characteristics, patents, trademarks, or technological advances
- Why is the company's product or service better, what does it do better than its competitors??

6.7 Pricing Strategy

- Describe the company's pricing strategy
- What does a product or service cost to produce?
- Research and document the cost factors
- Will special molds or equipment have to be built to manufacture your product?

6.8 Distribution Strategy

- What channels of distribution will the company use to get the products and services to market? Direct sales to the end user or wholesale B2B?
- License the products and services?
- Are there any supply problems or barriers to entry?
- Any special licensing required?

6.9 Promotion and Advertising Strategy

- What methods will the company use to communicate to customers that the products and services are available?
- Online or off-line?

6.10 Sales and Sales Force Strategies

- Outsourced sales representatives or an in-house sales force
- Commissioned or salaried?

6.11 Service Strategy

- How and where will the services will be delivered

7. Marketing Tactics and Action Plans

- Describe your marketing tactics and your action plans to implement your strategies

7.1 Products and Services
7.2 Pricing
7.3 Place - distribution
7.4 Promotions
7.5 People
7.6 Process
7.7 Physical evidence
7.8 Etc.
7.9 Gantt chart

- To include action plans and timelines
- Could be in the appendix

8. Budgets and Timelines

8.1 Marketing Budget

- Sales forecasts
- Expenses forecasts
- Budget proforma

8.2 Timelines

- Implementation milestones
- Deadlines
- Marketing team
- Tasks and allocation
- Gantt Chart with timelines for each activity

9. Evaluation and Control

9.1 Monthly and Quarterly Objectives
- Evaluate performance against objectives
- Make changes, corrections and adjustments where necessary

9.2 Monthly and Quarterly Figures
- Evaluate figures against targets
- Make changes, corrections and adjustments where necessary

9.3 Measurement of Performance Against Targets
- Customer feedback
- Budgets
- Sales
- Market share
- Profitability of marketing activities

9.4 Comparison of Results Against Standards
- Evaluate performance against standards
- Make changes, corrections and adjustments where necessary

10. Contingency Plans

10.1 Outline Contingency Plans
- Risk assessment
- Insurance

10.2 Provisions for Action
- Response strategy and action plans
- Plan B

11. Appendices

2. THE MARKETING PLAN

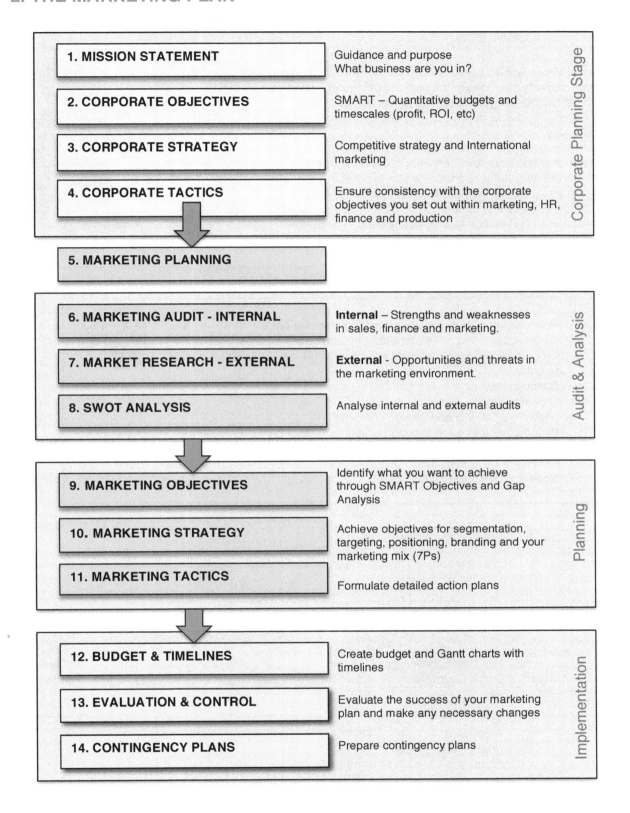

1. MISSION STATEMENT	Guidance and purpose What business are you in?
2. CORPORATE OBJECTIVES	SMART – Quantitative budgets and timescales (profit, ROI, etc)
3. CORPORATE STRATEGY	Competitive strategy and International marketing
4. CORPORATE TACTICS	Ensure consistency with the corporate objectives you set out within marketing, HR, finance and production

Corporate Planning Stage

5. MARKETING PLANNING

6. MARKETING AUDIT - INTERNAL	**Internal** – Strengths and weaknesses in sales, finance and marketing.
7. MARKET RESEARCH - EXTERNAL	**External** - Opportunities and threats in the marketing environment.
8. SWOT ANALYSIS	Analyse internal and external audits

Audit & Analysis

9. MARKETING OBJECTIVES	Identify what you want to achieve through SMART Objectives and Gap Analysis
10. MARKETING STRATEGY	Achieve objectives for segmentation, targeting, positioning, branding and your marketing mix (7Ps)
11. MARKETING TACTICS	Formulate detailed action plans

Planning

12. BUDGET & TIMELINES	Create budget and Gantt charts with timelines
13. EVALUATION & CONTROL	Evaluate the success of your marketing plan and make any necessary changes
14. CONTINGENCY PLANS	Prepare contingency plans

Implementation

Chapter 15 - CONCLUSION

1. YOUR CHALLENGES

The business environment is rapidly changing and more challenging than ever. Almost every business in the world is being influenced by significant changes, including rapid technological development, global competition, regulation to protect or liberalise competition and economic instability.

However, these changes and developments in the business environment are creating huge opportunities for businesses that are agile and capable of adapting to the effects of these changes. The winners will be the organisations, large or small, that actively apply fundamental marketing principles to their businesses – Ninja style!

FACT - THE ENVIRONMENT IS RAPIDLY CHANGING

- Political, economic, social and technological change
- Convergence and development of technologies
- E-commerce and the Internet offer new channels and reduce barriers to entry
- Social media
- Globalisation
- Growing domestic and foreign competition
- Rising customer sophistication which requires a higher level of quality, service and responsiveness
- Increased price sensitivity
- Shorter product life cycles

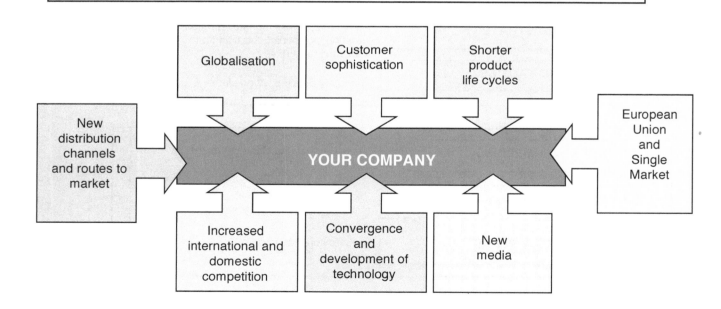

2. YOUR MARKETING PLAN

Now You're Ready to Create Your Own Marketing Plan

Creating your marketing plan is a modest investment of your resources in relation to the magnitude of the results that came come from successful marketing operations. Good marketing planning is vital to the success of your business. Be creative and innovate – create markets, don't just enter them.

The Ninja Marketer has the foresight to see where he wants to go, the best way to get there and how to ensure a successful arrival and to create and sustain a competitive advantage.

REMEMBER
Every journey begins with only one footstep and the steps you take today to plan and implement your marketing plan will help you to gain and sustain a long-term competitive advantage in the future.

Hi Ninja Marketer!

CONGRATULATIONS!!! You've earned your badge as a Ninja Marketer. We hope you enjoyed your journey through the Ninja Marketing Toolkit. We would love your feedback and really appreciate referrals.

Happy marketing! And we hope you'll join us for another exciting journey in our next books.

Lots of Ninja Love,
The Ninja Marketing Team and Princess Arielle

P.S.
You can contact Susan Lintell via email susanl7@me.com or contact us on our Facebook, Twitter and Linkedin pages. You can join our business network, www.prolinkconnection.com

Lightning Source UK Ltd.
Milton Keynes UK
UKHW050750211122
412560UK00008B/35

9 781910 266373